THE ● GREAT
TAX E$CAPE

Strategies for Early Planning and a **Lower Tax Bill**

FEATURING AMERICA'S TOP CERTIFIED TAX COACHES

FOREWORD BY **DOMINIQUE MOLINA, CPA, CTS**

ACKNOWLEDGEMENTS

Many thanks to all whose work, research, and support helped us to write this book. We especially want to thank the 115th Congress of the United States of America for arriving at a conclusion by adopting the 2017 Tax Cuts and Jobs Act on December 22, 2017. There has never been a better time to be a business taxpayer in this country, and as tax planners, the increase in tax breaks makes our work even more interesting and exciting as we familiarize ourselves with the new law.

Many hours of work went into the development, editing, design, and publishing to make this book possible. The authors would like to specifically thank Virginia Ruehrwein, Heidi Marttila-Losure, and Erikka Oxford, for their tireless efforts and many updates and changes to allow us to include the newest in tax law for our readers.

TABLE OF CONTENTS

CHAPTER 1

Planning Your Path Through the Tax Maze

Raymond Sawyer, EA, CTC

Getting through the maze of taxes is a complicated endeavor, and you will need every tool in your arsenal to succeed. In many cases, income and investments that appear to be strong at first glance turn out to be more expensive than expected once tax obligations are considered. Planning your way through the tax maze early can help you avoid the potential pitfalls along the way.

CHAPTER 2

Eliminating Unexpected Endings with a Profit-First Philosophy

Randy Owens EA, CTC, Certified Mastery Profit First Professional

50 percent of new businesses fail in the first year – and many more follow in their next few years of operation – which shows that plans for expansion are often unsuccessful. Understanding where failed companies went wrong – and how to avoid traveling the same path – is critical to your long-term success.

CHAPTER 16

Finding the Right Accountant to Successfully Guide You Through the Tax Maze

Joseph D. Rose, CPA, CTC

PAGE
185

Choosing an accountant takes time, and you might consider forgoing this process in favor of a do-it-yourself approach. However, most people who go this route end up regretting it for good reason: the tax savings they miss out on costs them much more money than a good accountant would have.

Foreword

DOMINIQUE MOLINA, CPA, CTS

I n Greek mythology the Labyrinth was an elaborate, confusing structure designed to hold a Minotaur, a deadly monster well feared by the community. The difficult maze served as a test for leaders, the best of whom could navigate its passages, slay the monster at the center and successfully find their way out again.

In the modern world, the tax code is not unlike a labyrinth. The Internal Revenue Code is a confusing maze of definitions and rules designed to reward successful business leaders while catching cheats and criminals in its jaws. Deep in its structure are the very things used by rich and famous companies to avoid taxes altogether – these companies successfully avoid the Minotaur and escape with even more wealth and power.

General Electric, one of the largest corporations in America, filed a whopping 57,000-page federal tax return, but didn't pay taxes on $14 billion in profits. The return, which was filed electronically, would have been 19 feet high if printed out and stacked (fortunately for tree lovers, the return was electronically filed). Yet every day small businesses struggle to cover a 37% tax bill, and by the time state, property, sales, and payroll taxes are added, business owners are lucky to have anything left to provide the very freedom that owning a business is supposed to bring.

The reason the wealthy pay less in tax is not because of how *much* money they earn. Rather it is because of *how* they earn it. The mythology of it all is that you must be rich to pay less in taxes, that the rich pay less in tax simply because they are rich. In reality, those that pay less in tax do so because they have knowledge; and they prioritize their funds in order to afford the right team of people who can provide the secrets to paying less.

When it comes to navigating the maze of tax accounting, few modern companies can match the depth of personnel GE hires for its tax department. What makes GE unusual, is that it is considered the largest employer of former Treasury employees. In fact, GE considers its tax strategy an essential part of its overall strategic plan for the health and growth of the business. One such example is its practice of recruiting dozens of former tax officials from Washington's official tax world. GE considers its tax department a profit center for the business and treats it accordingly.

How about you? Do you consider your tax portfolio a profit center for your business? Do you boldly enter the labyrinth and confidently face the Minotaur like GE, emerging with enough money to grow your wealth 24,000% faster?

You can do what the rich do by learning the map to legally navigate the code and safely defend yourself against the IRS by having a plan for keeping more of what you earn. Tax Planning is not just a map through the tax maze, it's like having someone hand you the keys to the hidden doors, allowing you to create your own path through the code. Opportunities and savings await at the end if you put in the effort of planning your route in advance. Owning a business provides the access and unlocks the door to limitless ideas for reducing your tax bill.

The authors of this book are some of the top professionals certified in tax planning; experts in the art of paying less tax. They are tax professionals who scour the tax code and thoroughly examine their client's income and business options to rescue every deduction, tax advantage, and credit possible from the IRS Minotaur. Certified Tax Coaches emphasize year-round proactive planning to ensure that business owners can utilize every available loophole and savings opportunity possible; and they've come together to share these secrets with you.

The strategies in this book will help teach you how to use the tax code to your advantage. No, you don't have to be a Fortune 100 company like General Electric or a billionaire like Buffett to pay very little in tax; you just need to plan your way through the maze.

To Your Financial Success,

Dominique Molina

Dominique Molina, CPA, CTS

The Tax Cuts and Jobs Act Overview

O n December 22, 2017, the largest tax reform in three decades, the Tax Cuts and Jobs Act, was passed. The article is dedicated to providing some guidance on the tax reform and aid in preparing for planning in 2018. The reform impacts individual and business taxes in 2017 and beyond. While much of the impact will be seen in 2018 through 2025, the changes could revert back to its current state if the future Congress does not extend the Act. That means that the individual tax changes would reset, and the tax law would return to the 2017 state that we all know of today.

For tax years 2018 through 2025, the changes present a number of year-end tax planning opportunities.

Individual Tax Implications

Income Tax Rate		Income Levels for Those Filing As:	
2017	2018-2025	Single	Married-Joint
10%	10%	$0-$9,525	$0-$19,050
15%	12%	$9,525-$38,700	$19,050-$77,400
25%	22%	$38,700-$82,500	$77,400-$165,000
28%	24%	$82,500-$157,500	$165,000-$315,000
33%	32%	$157,500-$200,000	$315,000-$400,000
33%-35%	35%	$200,000-$500,000	$400,000-$600,000
39.6%	37%	$500,000+	$600,000+

xvi The Great Tax Escape

Standard deduction – The Act increases the standard deduction through 2025.

- Single Filers – $6,500 to $12,000
- Married filing jointly – $13,000 to $24,000
- Heads of households – $9,500 to $18,000

Affordable Care Act – aka "Obamacare" – Repeals the penalty imposed on those who do not obtain insurance in 2019.

Personal Exemptions – Repeals all personal exemptions through 2025.

Itemized Deductions – The Act eliminates or restricts the ability to use several itemized deductions, through 2025.

State and Local Taxes OR Property Tax Deductions – Individuals are allowed a maximum deduction and must choose between state and local income or property taxes. Taxpayers cannot take a deduction in 2017 for prepaid 2018 state income taxes.

- Married filing jointly – $10,000
- Married filing separately – $5,000

Mortgage Interest – Limits the debt of the loan by filing status. Mortgages taken out or contracts entered into before Dec. 15 are still subject to the current tax laws.

- Married filing jointly – first $750,000

Home Equity Loans – Repealed through 2025.

Alternative Minimum Tax (AMT) – Raises the exemption amount and exemption phaseout threshold that was enacted to curb tax avoidance **among high earners**.

- **Married couples filing jointly** – Exemption increases to $109,400 and phaseout increases to $1,000,000.
- **All other taxpayers** – Exemption increases to $70,300 and phaseout increases to $500,000 (other than estates and trusts).

Casualty Losses – Applies only if the loss is attributable to a presidentially declared disaster.

Gambling Losses – The bill clarifies that the term "losses from wagering transactions" in Sec. 165(d) includes any otherwise allowable deduction incurred in carrying on a wagering transaction. This is intended to clarify that the limitation of losses from wagering transactions applies not only to the actual costs of wagers, but also to other expenses incurred by the taxpayer in connection with his or her gambling activity.

Charitable Contributions – The charitable contributions changes are limited or repealed.

- Increases the income-based percentage limit for charitable contributions of cash to public charities to 60%.
- Donations given in exchange for college seating tickets or athletics events are no longer allowed.

Miscellaneous Itemized Deductions – All miscellaneous itemized deductions subject to the 2% floor under current law are repealed through 2025.

Medical Expenses – Allows for medical expense deductions in excess of 7.5% of adjusted gross income for 2017 and 2018 for everyone not just those over the age of 65.

Child Tax Credit – The Act has several tax planning advantages.

- Increases the Child Tax Credit from $1,000 to $2,000 per child.
- The credit is refundable for qualifying taxpayers up to $1,400.
- Increases the maximum income level to qualify for the credit.
  - $400,000 for married taxpayers filing a joint return.
  - $200,000 for other taxpayers.
- Expansion of 529 savings plans.
  - Maximum distribution of $10,000 per student for tuition at private and religious K-12 schools.

- Allows parents to use the funds for expenses for home-schooled students.

IRA Recharacterizations – The Act repeals the ability to recharacterize one kind of IRA contribution as another, for example to designate a traditional contribution as a Roth contribution, or vice-versa.

Estate, Gift, and Generation-Skipping Transfer Taxes – This change will be reversed as of 2026.

The estate tax doubles the exemption and applies to estates of decedents dying and gifts made after Dec. 31, 2017, and before Jan. 1, 2026.

- $11.2 million for singles
- $22.4 million for couples

Other Credits – The Act repeals several tax credits.

- Credit for the elderly and permanently disabled.
- Credit for plug-in electric drive motor vehicles.
- Credit for interest on certain home mortgages.

Other Deduction Changes – The Act outlines other impacts to the individual taxpayer.

- **Alimony** – Alimony and separate maintenance payments are not deductible by the payor spouse and conversely not includible income by the payee spouse.
- **Moving Expenses** – Repealed for most with one major exception.
  - Members of the armed forces on active duty who move because of military orders or a change in where the member is stationed.
- **Exclusion for Bicycle Commuting Reimbursements** – The bill repeals through 2025 the exclusion from gross income or wages of qualified bicycle commuting expenses.

Business Tax Implications

For tax years beginning after Dec. 31, 2017, and beginning before Jan. 1, 2026, the Tax Reform and Jobs Act include the following changes that impact businesses.

Alternative Minimum Tax (AMT): Eliminated for corporations.

Income from Pass-Through Entities: The Act dramatically changes how individuals are taxed on income from partnerships, S corporations, and other pass-through entities.

- Increases deductions to 20% of "qualified business income" from a partnership, S corporation, or sole proprietorship.
  - "Qualified business income" means the net amount of qualified items of income, gain, deduction, and loss with respect to the qualified trade or business of the taxpayer.
  - Items must be conducted trade or business within the United States. They do not include specified investment-related income, deductions, or losses.
  - "Qualified business income" does not include an S corporation shareholder's reasonable compensation, guaranteed payments, or—to the extent provided in regulations—payments to a partner who is acting in a capacity other than his or her capacity as a partner.
  - "Specified service trades or businesses" include any trade or business in the fields of accounting, health, law, consulting, athletics, financial services, brokerage services, or any business where the principal asset of the business is the reputation or skill of one or more of its employees.
  - The exclusion from the definition of a qualified business for specified service trades or businesses phases in for a taxpayer with taxable income:
    - Singles – $157,500
    - Married filing jointly – $315,000

- Allowed deductions of 20% of qualified real estate investment trust (REIT) dividends, qualified cooperative dividends, and qualified publicly traded partnership income. (Special rules apply to specified agricultural or horticultural cooperatives.)
- Limitation on deduction based on W-2 wages above a threshold amount of taxable income, generally limited to 50%.
- Deduction disallows for specified service trades or businesses with income above a threshold.
- For each qualified trade or business, can deduct 20% of the qualified business income with respect to such trade or business.
- Capital-intensive businesses may yield a higher benefit under a rule that takes into consideration 25% of wages paid plus a portion of the business's basis in its tangible assets.

Corporate Income Tax Rate Reduction: The Act reduces the corporate income tax rate and expands property definitions.

- Reduces tax rate beginning in 2018 to 21 percent from 35 percent.
- Allows 100 percent expensing for business property placed in service after September 27, 2017 to encourage more capital investing in corporations
- Expands eligible property definition for 100 percent expensing, to include used property that was not previously used by the taxpayer. Expires in 2023 or 2024 for certain property.

International Tax Reform: The Act makes significant changes to the U.S. international tax code.

- Entirely replaces the current foreign subsidiaries system with a dividend exemption system. U.S. corporations are exempt from U.S. income tax for foreign-source dividends and certain foreign subsidiaries are exempt from U.S. income tax.
- Requires foreign subsidiaries to pay a repatriation tax on their foreign subsidiaries' post-1986 earnings and profits.

- Tax is 14.5 percent on foreign earnings held in cash and cash equivalents.
- 7.5 percent on foreign earnings held in illiquid assets.
- Imposes current U.S. income tax on 50 percent of foreign controlled corporation. Under the system, multinationals are taxed on foreign earned income.

Carried Interest: The Act addresses the tax of "carried interest," directed at private equity fund managers, hedge fund managers, and some other investment professionals to pay long-term capital gains rates on their share of the profits from an investment partnership.

- Beginning 2019, long-term capital gains attributable to an "applicable partnership interest" are characterized as short-term capital gain (taxable at ordinary income rates) to the extent applicable to an investment held less than three years.
- An applicable partnership interest generally means a partnership interest transferred about the performance of substantial services. In effect, the provision does not allow fund managers to benefit from the lower tax rate applicable to long-term capital gains unless the investment that generated the gain was held for at least three years.

Liquor Tax: The Act cuts taxes on beer, wine, and liquor.

One thing is clear: The tax reform plan will mean different things to different people, depending on how much they make, where they live, and their family size and makeup. See your tax planning professional for the best tax implementation plan for you, your family, and your business. The implications could have both negative and positive effects, so get the facts for your circumstances and ensure you escape the tax increase!

CHAPTER 1

Planning Your Path Through the Tax Maze

BY RAYMOND SAWYER, EA, CTC

N avigating the tax maze can be challenging, especially when your goal is to come out with your wealth intact. Planning ahead gives you an opportunity to map every move well in advance so you can be sure you aren't paying too much in taxes. Create a comprehensive blueprint that considers current and potential future sources of income, and be prepared to tweak your strategy when appropriate so you can reach your goals.

Choosing the Right Partner to Guide You Through the Tax Maze

Getting through the maze of taxes is a complicated endeavor, and you will need every tool in your arsenal to succeed. It requires understanding the specific tax issues that impact your situation as well as the strategies that will keep your tax bills low in the short-term so you can build long-term wealth. Although many investors rely on accountants and investment managers to provide advice on these topics, the truth is that these professionals typically do not have the specialized knowledge to guide you through the tax maze. Their goal is generally to increase your income and reduce your taxes in the current year, rather than creating a comprehensive strategy that will serve you in the long-term.

Consider enlisting the expertise of a Certified Tax Coach when creating your map. Skilled tax coaches know the nuances in the tax code, and they will be able to guide you in the best direction for your business. Remember, your income and investments will continue to grow, and even a relatively small reduction in the tax percentage you pay can be significant. Instead of handing more money over to Uncle Sam, you can reduce or defer some of your taxes so you can save and invest those funds instead.

A Certified Tax Coach is uniquely qualified to manage aspects of your financial profile that accountants, business advisors, and portfolio managers overlook. These tax professionals review your information from a unique perspective, focusing on the tax implications of your financial decisions. While taking your investment preferences, sources of income, and family obligations into consideration, these professionals work with you to create a comprehensive tax-minimization strategy.

The secret to maximizing your tax savings is to provide your Certified Tax Coach with as much information as possible. Sometimes sharing minor details can lead to big savings. Discuss your current businesses, the investments you already have, your financial obligations, and any work you do—both paid and unpaid—with your coach, and be prepared to examine nontraditional and unexpected routes through the tax maze.

Study Your Strengths and Opportunities Before Making Your Map

A shocking number of people forward all their financial documents to accountants and financial planners without even reviewing them. Many have minimal knowledge of their financial situation and depend on others to provide a summary. This is a grave mistake. While advice from professional financial guides is helpful, the best way to successfully navigate the tax maze is to begin with intimate knowledge of your finances before presenting your unique circumstances to a Certified Tax

Coach, who will then advise you on the best tax strategy for your business.

Start with a thorough self-evaluation. Examine all the following bits of information, and consult with experts if anything is unclear. You should walk away from this exercise with a full understanding of your complete financial profile, including your:

- Investments
- Sources of income
- Personal assets
- Personal expenses
- Business assets
- Business expenses
- Short-term financial obligations
- Long-term financial obligations

It would be a valuable exercise to estimate the tax rates on your investments and income. When you work through your financial plan later, this information can assist you in determining where your returns are greatest. In many cases, income and investments that appear to be strong at first glance turn out to be more expensive than expected once tax obligations are considered.

Think carefully about your history and personal preferences, and be prepared to discuss the following with your tax professional:

- What were your most significant financial errors and why did they happen?
- What were your greatest financial successes and how did they happen?
- What are your short-term financial goals?
- What are your long-term financial goals?
- What does financial success look like to you?
- What lifestyle changes are you willing to make to realize your financial goals?

- How much risk are you willing to take?
- What is your idea of an ideal tax planning strategy?

Ensure that your list is comprehensive and includes potential expenses and obligations, including those that are far-off in the future. Your long-term financial strategy should consider your retirement, and you should have a plan in place if you experience serious health issues, including partial or complete disability.

Examining these subjective questions is critical to finding an investment and tax strategy that will work for you. For example, families with children may have college expenses to consider, while individuals with a chronic illness must factor in medical costs. These immediate needs and long-term goals require different investment and tax strategies for maximum effect.

An honest look at your current lifestyle—and what you are willing to do without—will impact your rate of savings and investment. If you place high importance on fine dining and designer clothes, it isn't sensible to make a financial plan that excludes these kinds of luxuries. While you may be successful in temporarily cutting them out of your spending habits, you are unlikely to abandon such desires long term. Your financial plan should include a realistic picture of your lifestyle.

Financial success looks different to everyone, and your passions will drive your measures of success. For some, success will be financial independence, living off investment income and traveling the world. For others, a certain lifestyle is the dream, perhaps a waterfront home with enough disposable income to buy and maintain a boat. Some people have a certain dollar figure in mind, while others have a burning desire to see their investments grow exponentially throughout their lifetime. Some individuals endeavor to leave behind the largest possible financial legacy to their families. Whatever your situation, the goal is to work with your Certified Tax Coach to create a plan that takes your true goals into consideration.

Other important considerations in a comprehensive financial plan include the following:

- What market trends will impact your business (favorably or unfavorably) in the short-term?
- What market trends will impact your business (favorably or unfavorably) in the long-term?
- Have you been tracking increases and decreases in value-based equity? What trends do you see?
- What will your cash flow needs be in different market scenarios?
- What benchmarks can you identify to track whether your financial strategy is successful?

As you consider your next steps, remember that the greater the risk, the greater your potential reward will be—but losses are just as likely. Decisions you make regarding the risk/reward balance will have a long-term impact on your overall financial well-being. Your strategy must consider risks such as reduced value of passive investments, lost value due to inflation, major life changes, currency devaluation, and significant market swings. Generally speaking, the longer your investment time frame, the more risk you can afford to take. When you can't afford to take risks, diversification and certain insurance products can help.

Avoiding the Capital Gains Detour

Watching the success of your investments and the increasing value of your assets is supremely satisfying, until you are ready to liquidate. Suddenly, you may discover that your success is punished by a hefty tax bill. Fortunately, there are methods to safely avoid the capital gains detour, as long as you plan ahead with your tax professional. For example, you can reduce capital gains taxes by offsetting them in years when your tax bracket is lower or you have other investment losses.

Other common situations—and their solutions—include the following:

1. **Matching gains and losses** – Capital gains and losses can balance each other out when they occur in the same tax year. In certain situations, you can offset up to $3,000 in regular income,

and the unused loss can be carried over into the next tax year to offset further capital gains.

2. **Tax-deductible charitable contributions** – With the right strategy in place, your annual giving can save you capital gains taxes. In this case, you are required to gift appreciated stock to the nonprofit of your choice instead of cash. You can still deduct the full value of the stock, but you never realize capital gains for tax purposes, which reduces your overall tax liability.

3. **Choosing your primary residence with tax advantages in mind** – Typically, purchasing real estate, improving it, and selling it for a profit results in significant capital gains taxes, but there is an exception. If the property you are flipping is your primary residence, you do not have to pay taxes on capital gains of up to $250,000 for an individual or $500,000 for a married couple. Choosing to live in the property while you renovate can result in significant savings.

4. **Retirement savings accounts** – The government is committed to encouraging individuals to save for their retirement, and a number of programs have been developed to make saving easier and less expensive. Traditional IRA and 401(k) programs offer tax-deferred savings. You don't pay any taxes until you take distributions, and you can time your distributions to ensure maximum savings.

5. **Health savings accounts** – Encouraging individuals to save for expenses associated with health care is another high priority for government agencies. As a result, many people are now eligible for health savings accounts. While there is a limit to the amount you can contribute, your contributions and earnings are tax-free.

6. **Reinvestment** – When you realize significant capital gains, you have a choice: you can take the cash, invest in a different type of asset, or invest in a similar type of asset. Investing capital gains into a similar asset within 180 days is referred to as a 1031 Exchange. By selecting the 1031 Exchange method, you are not liable for capital gains tax on the initial sale.

7. **Leaving investments untouched for your beneficiaries** – If you intend to leave certain investments to your beneficiaries, there is no need to sell in advance of your death. Your beneficiaries are unlikely to pay capital gains taxes on investment growth, because the cost basis for the investment will match its current value when ownership is transferred.

8. **Gifting appreciated investments** – When you are in a high tax bracket, you may discover that selling an appreciated asset is not particularly worthwhile. However, that same investment could be quite valuable to a family member in a lower tax bracket. In this situation, consider gifting appreciated investments to family members who will pay capital gains taxes based on your original cost but at their tax rates.

Capital gains taxes are some of the most insidious. They rapidly diminish the value of appreciation of assets and investments you have worked hard to realize. These strategies can reduce the amount of capital gains taxes you pay, protecting the value of your investment.

Overcoming Tax Roadblocks Through Trusts

As any financial planner will tell you, trusts are the safest way to protect the value of your estate for your heirs. They typically reduce the amount of estate taxes assessed and allow for the avoidance of probate expenses. They permit assets to be transferred to beneficiaries without attorney's fees and court costs, dramatically reducing expenses charged to the estate.

Trusts also serve to hold assets for one or more beneficiaries. They come in a variety of forms, and each can be customized to the individual needs of your estate and your family. When creating a trust, you have the opportunity to specify its terms in detail so that you continue to control your assets. Many investors are concerned that beneficiaries are ill prepared to manage estate proceeds responsibly and effectively. Fortunately, trusts can be tailored to address that very issue, specifying when funds will be released, under what circumstances they can be withheld, and at what rate they can be accessed. Popular structures include trusts to provide for surviving spouses and children, and skip-generation trusts to provide for grandchildren.

These are some of the most important terms to be aware of when considering a trust:

- **"A" trust** – Designed to provide funds to your surviving spouse immediately, without the delays and expenses associated with probate.
- **"B" trust** – Designed to bypass a surviving spouse's estate so that there is no estate tax liability.
- **Revocable trust** – You have the option to remove assets from this type of trust, which limits some of the tax benefits.
- **Irrevocable trust** – Assets are permanently removed from your estate to the ownership of the beneficiaries via the trust. You will not be responsible for taxes on these assets. This is an effective way to reduce your tax burden from assets that are rapidly increasing in value.

The Critical Role of Life Insurance

Understanding the basics of life insurance and the role these products play in building wealth can make a substantial difference in your family's long-term financial security. All too often, simple lack of knowledge results in serious life insurance related missteps that are difficult to correct.

The less expensive and more commonly held life insurance product is term life, which provides financial security in case of your death during the period specified by the policy. Most individuals purchase this product during their working years, when they are responsible for the support of young children and their bills include large expenses like a mortgage or outstanding student loans. However, at the end of the term, the policy has no value. None of the premiums paid into the policy are returned, and it is essentially as if the policy never existed at all.

Whole life is an entirely different type of product, which operates more like an investment than an insurance policy. While it provides financial security for your family in case of your death, it also has intrinsic value, unlike term life. Your whole life policy builds cash value that you can borrow against, and it can be used to establish a trust. These life insurance trusts permit heirs to access funds quickly so that they can easily pay estate taxes and keep up payments on basic living and business expenses. When paired with an irrevocable trust, estate taxes are reduced and wealth is transferred to heirs without the time and expense of probate.

Taking a Deeper Dive Into the Tax Implications of Retirement Programs

The regulations around retirement savings accounts are designed to save you money in taxes, and a combination of strategies will maximize your ability to realize these advantages. However, care must be taken in the distribution phase. Work with your Certified Tax Coach to ensure that your distributions will not erase potential tax savings.

When deciding whether to take a distribution from your retirement account, the first step is to estimate your tax rate. You can do this by examining your income, expenses and loan obligations for the year, as well as the tax deductions and exemptions you expect to qualify for. Determine your adjusted gross income as closely as possible to estimate your tax rate.

If you are in the 15 percent bracket, taking a withdrawal from tax-deferred retirement accounts like a traditional IRA or 401(k) to close any gaps between income and expenses protects your tax savings. Your withdrawal should keep you within the range of adjusted gross income that qualifies you for a 15 percent tax bracket, or else you will find yourself spending more in tax expenses. If you need more than the amount that would put your adjusted gross income over the 15 percent tax bracket, withdraw from your Roth IRA instead; these funds are distributed tax-free.

Another tax benefit you may be entitled to is tax-free capital gains from qualified dividends provided you are in the 10 percent or 15 percent tax bracket, up to a maximum of $75,900 in 2017 for married couples. Managing distributions from retirement accounts can be tricky, but the tax savings makes this project well worth your attention.

A New Look at Estate Planning

After a lifetime of careful saving and investing, you want to be sure your estate passes on to your beneficiaries intact. Without planning ahead for disposal of your estate, it is likely that a significant amount will be lost to taxes. At one time, estate taxes reached almost 50 percent of the total value. Today, there are new opportunities available through the American Taxpayer Relief Act of 2012, which increased the amount exempted from estate taxes to $5.43 million and created a combined estate and gift tax rate of 40 percent.

Prior to 2012, many investors paid little attention to minimizing tax liability in areas such as capital gains taxes. This was not a priority, as capital gains taxes were lower than expected estate taxes. However, with the increased exemption, more people are able to avoid estate taxes, which brings renewed attention to tax minimization strategies. Now smart investors are carefully considering which assets to retain and which to sell. With the right strategy, capital gains and other taxes can be minimized, and more of the estate can be kept below the $5.43 million exemption ceiling.

Relying on Guides to Maximize Savings and Minimize Taxes

Getting through the tax maze with your wealth intact requires a team of professionals to guide you through complex laws and regulations. Choose a Certified Tax Coach as well as a highly qualified financial planner and investment advisor to ensure that your selections fit your lifestyle, risk tolerance, and financial goals.

Most important, keep in mind that your financial plan and tax-minimizing strategy are fluid, living documents. As your life circumstances and goals change, so will your overall financial picture. Keep your team informed of major life events. The following can dramatically impact your financial situation:

- Birth, adoption, or death of a child
- Marriage
- Divorce
- Death of a spouse
- Child entering or graduating from college
- Natural disaster impacting business or personal property
- Accident, injury, disability, diagnosis of disease
- Purchase of a home
- Sale of a home
- Loss of a job
- New job
- Inheritance

Remember, the events that are important in your life are important to your Certified Tax Coach and financial professionals. Stay in touch with your team to discuss changing circumstances, and regularly review your plans to ensure they still fit your needs and the needs of your family.

ABOUT THE AUTHOR

Raymond Sawyer, EA, CTC

Raymond Sawyer is an Enrolled Agent, Certified Tax Coach and a Realtor. He founded Sawyer One Stop Accounting and Tax in 2008. Mr. Sawyer received his undergraduate degree of Bachelor of Business Administration with a focus in accounting with distinction, and he has been saving people money on their taxes ever since.

Mr. Sawyer's primary objective as an accountant and tax planner is to build personalized, quality relationships with his clients to be able to best serve them. He takes the time to understand each client's personal situation and business so that he is able to design the best strategic tax plan for each one. The goal of each plan is to reduce or eliminate tax liability long-term. Mr. Sawyer will ensure that you receive every tax break available to you, while also maintaining the utmost integrity in your return. You can count on his recommendations to always be in line with the current tax code.

As an Enrolled Agent, Mr. Sawyer has earned the privilege of representing taxpayers before the Internal Revenue Service. With his proven track record, you can be assured that your case is in good hands. Mr. Sawyer protects his clients' interests while helping them meet their current and future business goals.

Sawyer One Stop Accounting and Tax is based on one simple principle: Always do what is in the best interests of the client. While the company provides a variety of services, the common thread is that nothing is more important than each client's personal and business goals and objectives.

Mr. Sawyer was born and raised in Southern California with his four siblings. He currently lives in Fullerton, CA, with his wife and daughter.

It is important for him to give back to the community in which he lives and works. A long time volunteer for various charitable causes, he was awarded the Frank Palko Humanitarian Award in 2005. It is his continued goal to be a positive example to his family and to the community in which he lives.

To better suit your needs, Sawyer One Stop Accounting and Tax offers consultations in person, over the phone or web based. Please contact the office at (562) 690-2181 or SawyerOneStop@SawyerOneStop.com to see how the firm may be able to be of assistance to you, your family, or your business.

Comedian Fred Allen once said, "An income tax form is like a laundry list—either way you lose your shirt." If you stop at One Stop, you can be sure this won't happen to you!

Accounting Services offered but not limited to:

- Tax Return Preparation
- IRS & State Representation
- Audits, Correspondence Examinations
- Real Estate Sales, Purchases, & Financing
- IRS and State Settlement Agreements
- Strategical Tax Analysis
- Extreme Tax Reduction or Elimination
- IRS & State Payment Plans
- Payroll, Employer Tax Returns & Tax Deposits
- Bookkeeping & General Accounting

CHAPTER 2

Eliminating Unexpected Endings with a Profit-First Philosophy

BY RANDY OWENS EA, CTC, CERTIFIED MASTERY PROFIT FIRST PROFESSIONAL

For many entrepreneurs, opening their doors or going live online is the proudest moment of their lives. All of the planning that goes into creating a business has paid off, and the product or service that started as an idea is launched into the marketplace. Typically, the next goal is growth: business owners focus on marketing to consumers, expanding their reach, and turning a small company into a major player. Unfortunately, 50 percent of new businesses fail in the first year of operation, and many more follow in their next few years, making it clear that plans for expansion are frequently unsuccessful. Often, this is caused by a business owners' failure to put the same emphasis on minimizing business taxes, increasing revenue, and creating profits as they do with their personal finances. Understanding where failed companies went wrong—and how to avoid traveling the same path is critical to your long-term success.

The Risks of a Revenue-First Strategy

Almost every issue of popular entrepreneur and investment publications includes profiles of wildly successful businesses. The rags-to-riches story is an American favorite, and writers are quick to share images of start-ups that are transforming their industries and innovators who are disrupting decades of corporate tradition. Because the organizations being profiled have rocketed from almost nothing to massive revenue, the obvious assumption is that someone is getting rich. Unfortunately, that's not always, or even usually, true.

Businesses usually operate on a revenue-first philosophy, creating strategic plans that are focused on landing the next big client or the next major investor. This rapid growth requires constant cash infusion, which is oftentimes only made possible with loans, credit cards, and other forms of debt. Many companies that appear to be on the fast track are managing cash flow week-to-week and check-to-check. Their financial health is an illusion, and they learn too late that the only way to stay solvent is for sales to remain steady or increase.

A reduction in sales means an inability to get critical bills paid, and an increase in sales brings a series of complex problems driven by typical human behavior. While the cash flows in, business owners spend, either to continue expanding the business or to improve their lifestyles. Sometimes both. Sadly, sales are cyclical in nature, and boom periods will always be followed by a lull. After taking on the additional expenses that come with a larger organization or more elaborate lifestyle, a decline in sales that lasts longer than expected will leave you scrambling to cover your bills. All too often, businesses that appear profitable on the outside are without resources to manage cash flow, which causes them to fold. These organizations failed to put profit first.

The Basics of a Profit-First© Philosophy

The accounting formula for profitability is one of the first lessons business owners learn: Sales – Expenses = Profit. However, an over-reliance on this method of calculating profits causes many companies to fail. With this formula, profit comes last, which is the exact opposite of true financial health. Instead, author Michael Michalowicz follows a different formula, one which may be arguably one of the greatest business hacks of all time. Mike proposes a "profit-first© philosophy," which takes another look at managing expenses and cash flow by incorporating profit-driven methodology into every aspect of business operations. Instead of leaving profits as an afterthought, owners of profit-first businesses come out on top.

Putting profits first requires a new formula to manage the inflow and outflow of cash: Sales – Profit = Expenses. Instead of spending freely to encourage business growth and letting profits fall where they may, this formula guarantees your business will be profitable with every transaction. You naturally begin to spend on expansion within a tight budget that ensures long-term sustainable growth.

Letting go of the constant drive to grow your company can be difficult, but the rewards are well worth your effort. Instead of maintaining a huge company that is constantly threatening to collapse in on itself, you will enjoy the peace of mind of a smaller, financially sound business that can continue to provide you with income indefinitely. The following four principles will quickly get you on the road to operating under a profit-first philosophy.

Profit-First Principle #1: Smaller Plates

According to Michalowicz, the weight loss industry has made a fortune studying eating behaviors, then packing research findings into a variety of diet and nutrition programs. Smart entrepreneurs understand that this research applies to far more than the relationship between people and food. Many facets of human behavior—such as eating or exercise habits, for example—provide the foundation for relationships with a variety of lifestyle elements. Accordingly, behaviors that have been proven to support weight loss are also effective in other areas, including operating the financial side of a business.

Researchers spent a lot of time trying to understand why people ignore signals from their bodies that tell them to stop eating. One of the most profound discoveries is plate size. From infancy on, Americans are generally encouraged to finish all of the food on their plates, and larger plates lead to larger portions. By simply serving food on smaller plates, people are far less likely to overeat.

Michalowicz's idea is to use the smaller plate strategy and apply it to operating a profitable business. Simply reducing the size of the "plates" inspires business owners to be more frugal with spending. The traditional method of managing finances brings all income into an account, and decisions about where and how to allocate spending are made by the size of the account. When there are large amounts of cash available, it is far too easy to overspend—much like the tendency to overeat when food fills a large plate.

The profit-first philosophy creates new habits for managing cash flow that prevent overspending when income accounts have a hefty balance. Instead, every penny that comes into the business is periodically dispersed to smaller "plates" or subsidiary accounts. The amount allocated to each subsidiary account is predetermined by percentage, and each one has a specific purpose. Most people start with five foundational accounts, adding more as needed: Income, Owner Compensation, Profit, Taxes, and Operating Expenses.

Profit-First Principle #2: Serve Sequentially

Nutrition specialists know that sequencing meals matters, but you don't need a degree to understand that serving dessert first is a mistake. Starting with low-nutrition/high-calorie items results in very little appetite for foods that are full of vitamins and minerals that keep the body operating at full capacity. Nutrition specialists and dieticians encourage deliberate sequencing of meals, front-loading every food experience with the most nutrient-dense items on the menu. Through sequencing, you can achieve nutritional balance with every meal.

When it comes to managing your company's finances, "serving sequentially" can make a dramatic impact. Instead of paying bills first, then taking stock of what's left to make decisions about expansion and profit, make sure you stick to your program of allocating the pre-determined percentage of all income to the appropriate account.

Consider the effect this will have on your spending habits: Instead of putting your first effort into paying your bills, you "ration your appetite" to ensure you taste a bit of everything. If you don't have enough money to pay all of your expenses, you don't take it from other accounts. You focus on getting your expenses down to the point where you can comfortably pay them without creating hardships in other financial areas.

Profit-First Principle #3: Remove Temptation

Cupboards stocked with high-calorie snacks and freezers full of ice cream offer easy access to diet cheats when motivation is low. A single moment of stress can quickly translate into 2,000 calories. Weight loss programs make this one of their top refrains: get temptation out of the house. You are far less likely to make the effort required to obtain your guilty pleasures if they aren't readily available.

The same principle applies to keeping your business on the right financial track: focus on profits instead of constant, unsustainable expansion. Remove temptation by making it much more difficult to tap into profit accounts when you get nervous about covering expenses. If you set up these accounts in such a way that transferring or withdrawing requires time and effort, you are far more likely to come up with an alternative, profit-first solution. More importantly, if these accounts aren't constantly visible, you are less likely to think of them when you get into a financial bind. Out of sight is truly out of mind.

Profit-First Principle #4: Enforce a Rhythm

The reason why regular meals are a tenet of weight loss programs is simple. Good habits lead to better outcomes. When you eat on a schedule, your body grows accustomed to the rhythm, and you find it easier to eat reasonable portions of healthier foods than if you take a more haphazard, unprepared approach.

All people have a story about waiting too long to eat. Hunger got the better of them, and they ravenously devoured a huge amount of unhealthy food: a whole pizza, an entire package of cookies, or maybe sixteen portions of crackers and cheese. Getting out of a routine translated to neglecting their needs until the situation became critical, and then they made bad decisions.

Rhythm and habit are helpful in managing finances for the same reason. By handling your accounts based on habit and routine, you avoid a crisis mode that results in overspending or allocating funds to the wrong areas of your business. Sales cycles are standard in every industry, and your company is sure to have periods of high revenue followed by periods when sales slump. If you stick with your financial rhythm, you won't be tempted to spend too much when cash seems abundant, leaving nothing for lean times.

Choose a funds transfer schedule that makes sense based on your business, perhaps weekly, biweekly, or monthly. Transfer income to your foundation accounts on this schedule, regardless of sales during that period. Since your allocation is based on percentages, the actual dollar amount doesn't impact your financial management habits. Once you have made the appropriate transfers, it's time to pay your bills. Thanks to your regular handling of income and expenses, you will gain a clear picture of where your cash comes from and where it goes.

Why the Profit-First Philosophy Works

Human nature is quirky, and entrepreneurs have an opportunity to let those quirks run amok with the business or to harness their power and use them to create a profit-first enterprise. The first trick of human nature is Parkinson's Law: Work expands so as to fill the time available for its completion. Philosopher Cyril Northcote Parkinson articulated this rule in a 1955 essay he wrote for the Economist. Others have since added their own corollaries, including these words of wisdom:

- Stock–Sanford – If you wait until the last minute, it only takes a minute to do.
- Horstman – Work contracts to fit in the time we give it.
- Asimov – In ten hours a day you have time to fall twice as far behind your commitments as in five hours a day.

The basic premise is this: The demand upon a resource tends to expand to match the supply of the resource if the price is zero. Two of an entrepreneur's most valuable resources are time and money. You can count on the fact that your growth will eat up as much or as little of both as you permit. By taking profits out first, then focusing on your expenses, you are far more likely to pare down on unnecessary costs and come up with innovative solutions for saving money.

A second quirk also applies to the profit-first philosophy: The Primacy Effect. Essentially, this law of human nature says that we place additional significance on whatever we encounter first. Consider how this principle influences the outcome of the two possible accounting perspectives, Sales – Expenses = Profit versus Sales – Profit = Expenses. In the traditional version, profits are an afterthought. The Primacy Effect keeps focus on sales and profit. In the Profit-First model, your attention remains focused on sales and profits, making it far more likely that profits will stay on the top of your priority list.

Creating a business that can succeed long-term requires a model that can support growth and profitability. Unfortunately, many startups never find this balance. They place too much focus on growth, investing resources past the point where they can recover from the endless cycle of debt. Successful businesses balance growth and expansion with a healthy focus on profits. They take profits out of the income pool before there is a temptation to overspend. This requires them to limit expenses to what they can reasonably afford, creating a business model that grows at a sustainable pace.

For more information on applying the Profit First Strategy in your business, I recommend reading, "Profit First: A Simple System to Transform Any Business" by author and expert Mike Michalowicz. The next step is to meet with a Certified Profit First Professional, like me, who can help you implement Mike's strategies. Let's schedule an in-person or phone meeting to discuss how this model will help you get paid first in your business.

ABOUT THE AUTHOR

Randal Owens, EA, CTC, Certified Mastery Profit First Professional

What if your business served you, rather than you serving your business?

Randy Owens works primarily with owners of service-based and professional businesses who are dedicated to the health and prosperity of their businesses. They love what they do but are sometimes overwhelmed by the day-to-day responsibilities that come with it, taking time from their passion. Through the Profit First System, the professionals and

business owners working with Randy use a counterintuitive cash management system that helps them improve their profitability from the beginning.

Randy is totally committed to helping his clients look at their taxes and finances in a way that their more traditional accountant or bookkeeper would have never thought of. Just this one change in viewing things differently than the masses can almost instantly transform your business to a profit machine.

Through Financial Connections, the business he founded in Orange County, California, Randy Owens works with and guides entrepreneurs and independent professionals with their profit, tax, and bookkeeping needs so that they can concentrate on doing what they love without losing their sanity. Improving and maximizing their profit allows them the freedom to do what they love. Financial Connections is also pretty darn good at taxes and bookkeeping (though you should expect that!). Randy's entrepreneurial journey started back in junior high/high school when he started out delivering newspapers. Later, after stints in banking and as an investment professional, Randy grew dissatisfied with the restrictions of large organizations and set out on his entrepreneurial path in this business. His experience in life as a business owner makes him uniquely qualified to share the path to business success and avoid or overcome the potholes that come along the way.

Randy can be reached at 714-543-7884 or by email at Randy@FinConTax.com.

CHAPTER 3

Staying on Track: Finding Your Way to Tax Free Income

BY MERYL B. GREENWALD, CPA, CTC

M anaging your expenses to minimize your tax liability is a critical component of your tax saving strategy. However, maximizing deductions isn't the only tactic available to get through the tax maze successfully. In addition to a wide variety of strategies for deferring taxes on your income, examine opportunities for increasing the amount of tax-free income you receive. A combination of expense management, tax-deferral, and tax-free income can make an enormous difference in your overall tax obligations.

Mapping Investment Account Options

Investment accounts are an important income source, but heavy taxation can drastically reduce earnings. Understanding the types of investment accounts available—and how each is taxed—makes it easier to create a long-term plan to reduce tax liability.

Some of the most common account types also cost the most when it comes to taxes. You are required to pay on all of your earnings, whether or not you choose to make a withdrawal. In some cases, the increased value of your account falls under capital gains, while in others, your earnings are considered income. In either case, these programs can quickly become expensive. The following investment accounts offer you nothing in the way of tax advantages.

Standard Savings Accounts

Funds you keep in a standard savings account at your bank are essentially entirely liquid. You may be limited to a certain number of withdrawals or outgoing transfers per month, but the amount you withdraw is not restricted (though your bank may require a minimum monthly balance to avoid service fees). However, the price of this flexibility is very low rates of interest, typically under one percent. Savings account interest is reported on a 1099-INT form, and earnings are taxed as interest income. These accounts are FDIC insured up to $250,000, making them a safe choice for setting funds aside.

Money Market Accounts (MMA)

Many commercial banks offer money market accounts, which are similar in structure to standard savings accounts. The same transaction limits apply, and earnings are taxed as interest income. The primary difference is that your bank requires a higher minimum balance to avoid service fees, and the interest paid on your funds may be slightly higher than a standard savings account. These accounts are also FDIC insured, and earnings are taxed as interest income.

Certificates of Deposit

Better known as CDs, certificates of deposit represent an agreement between you and the bank. You agree to leave an amount of money in your account for a specified period of time, and your bank rewards you by paying a higher rate of interest than you would get in a standard checking or savings account. Usually, the longer you agree to leave funds in a CD, the higher the interest rate.

These accounts are FDIC insured, but in exchange for reduced risk, average interest rates are substantially lower than other types of investment accounts. If you choose to withdraw funds before the CD matures, the bank typically charges an interest penalty. The bank reports any interest you earn on a 1099-INT form, and your earnings are taxed as interest income.

Mutual Funds

Mutual funds provide an excellent way to diversify investments when you don't have a lot of money or you don't want to manage a large number of separate securities. You can purchase shares in a mutual fund, along with many other investors, and a fund manager makes all of the decisions about how to manage the group's money. Mutual funds have stated investment goals and strategies, so you can choose a fund based on your interests and needs. For example, some are entirely focused on international securities, while others invest in a specific industry. Still others have a broader focus, choosing a basket of shares of large cap and small cap—smaller and larger companies, respectively—in different industries.

The money you invest in a mutual fund is not FDIC insured, and you could lose part or all of your principal, which is the original amount of your investment. Your benefits come from the increased value of the mutual fund shares as underlying investments grow in value, as well as income from dividends paid on underlying investments. Your Certified Tax Coach is an important ally here, as you may be responsible for taxes on dividends, capital gains, or both.

Stock Trading Accounts

Some investors prefer to choose their own securities and they open stock trading accounts. Trades can be made by individual investors, or they may be left to investment advisors. There are many choices for stock trading accounts, ranging from fully managed by a professional to entirely self-managed through an online platform. Either way, stock trading accounts are not FDIC insured. Your tax liability depends on when and how you trade, as well as whether you realize gains or losses, and dividends. You may be responsible for taxes on dividends, capital gains, or both.

Tax-Advantaged Investment Options

For the average investor, none of the accounts previously listed offer tax savings, unless they are used in conjunction with a retirement program. Retirement accounts are specifically designed to grow your wealth by offering tax advantages, such as deferred assessment of income taxes and tax-free earnings. However, in order to enjoy these benefits, you have to meet certain eligibility requirements.

Deferring Taxes

Tax-deferred accounts don't erase tax liability, but they do put it off until you withdraw the funds. This gives you flexibility to strategically plan account distributions for years when your tax rate is lower, so you pay less in overall taxes. Investors have several options for tax-deferred accounts: traditional Individual Retirement Accounts (IRAs) and annuities are two of the most common.

Traditional IRAs

Traditional IRAs allow you to make contributions up to an annual limit, and you don't have to pay income tax on the amount you contribute in the year you make the contribution nor any of the income earned that year. Instead, you pay taxes on your contributions and subsequent earnings later, when you withdraw from the account. With a traditional IRA, you can choose to hold your savings in standard savings accounts, money market accounts, certificates of deposit, mutual funds, and/or stock trading accounts.

Annuities

Annuities may also be tax-deferred, though they work a little differently. These products are sold by life insurance companies, and they are intended to ensure that you don't have to worry about outliving your income. You can invest a lump sum or you can make payments over years—even decades—until you reach the agreed-upon total contribution. Depending on how you set up your annuity payments, you may receive income from this investment for life. In some cases, annuities can be used to provide beneficiaries with income once you have died.

Tax-deferred annuities allow you to delay paying taxes on the income that you contribute. Instead, you pay income tax when you receive distributions. For many, this lowers the overall amount of taxes paid, as many people find themselves in lower tax brackets after retirement.

Employer-Sponsored Retirement Programs

Many employers offer retirement savings options as part of a comprehensive benefits package. Individuals who are self-employed also have access to certain tax-advantaged retirement savings plans. The most common are tax-deferred retirement accounts, in which contributions are made with pre-tax income, and taxes are assessed on contributions and earnings when distributions are eventually taken.

401(k)

Larger organizations usually offer a 401(k), and they permit employees to make contributions directly from their paychecks. Often, companies match a portion of their employees' contributions in lieu of the nearly obsolete pension programs that employees used to receive. Employee contributions are made with pre-tax dollars, and employees pay taxes on their own contributions, their employers' contributions, and earnings only when distributions are taken.

SEP IRA

Smaller companies and sole proprietorships often choose the Simplified Employee Pension Individual Retirement Account (SEP IRA) program, which allows the business to make contributions on behalf of employees. This is especially popular with sole proprietors, because the business cannot just contribute to the business owner's account. If a deposit is made to any employee's account, the business must contribute to accounts for all eligible employees. Nevertheless, there are circumstances in which companies with a small number of employees will choose the SEP IRA.

Employer contributions are not taxed as employee income when the contributions are made. Instead, taxes are deferred, and the employees pay taxes on the employer's contributions and related earnings when they withdraw funds from the account.

SIMPLE IRA

The Savings Incentive Match Plan for Employees (SIMPLE IRA) is more common among small businesses with 100 employees or less. Employers and employees can contribute to employee accounts, and employers can choose to contribute a percentage of each employee's pay or match employee contributions up to a pre-set percentage. Employer and employee contributions, as well as account earnings, are tax-deferred, and employees must pay income taxes on the full amount of any distributions taken.

Solo 401(k)

Individuals who are self-employed and have no one working for them may prefer the Solo 401(k). It is quite similar to the 401(k) programs offered by large companies, but the self-employed individual and his or her spouse are the only participants. Contributions can come from the business owner's income or the business or both, and taxes are deferred until distributions are taken.

Because these programs offer special tax advantages, there are penalties for withdrawals taken before the participant reaches the age of 59 ½. Barring a limited number of special circumstances, the IRS will assess a 10 percent early withdrawal penalty, in addition to any other required income taxes. The special circumstances vary for IRA's vs 401(k) plans so you need to be very careful and heed the recommendations of a certified professional to ensure compliance.

Tax-Exempt Investment Options

Some investors prefer not to participate in tax-deferred programs, because they don't want to risk paying more taxes later due to an unexpected long-term increase in income, changes in the tax law, or other unpredictable events. However, keeping income taxes low is still a priority. These individuals typically invest in tax-exempt programs.

Contributions to tax-exempt accounts are made with after-tax dollars, and earnings grow tax-free. When you take withdrawals from tax-exempt accounts, you don't pay additional taxes on the funds you contributed, and there are no taxes assessed on earnings. This is true tax-free income.

Roth IRA

The Roth IRA program is a relative newcomer to the retirement planning field, and it offers an opportunity for investors to save for retirement without worrying about paying taxes in the future. Once a Roth IRA has been established, accounts housed under its umbrella can include any of the account types previously discussed, including standard savings accounts, money market accounts, certificates of deposit, mutual funds, and stock trading accounts.

Program participants make their contributions with after-tax dollars, up to an annual limit. Earnings grow entirely tax-free, and no taxes are due when distributions are taken. It is important to note that not everyone is eligible for a Roth IRA. The IRS sets an income cap, and if you make more than the specific amount, you cannot open a Roth IRA.

There is an exception to the tax-free earnings benefit. Outside of a narrow set of circumstances, any withdrawals taken before the age of 59 ½ are subject to taxes on the earnings related to the distribution amount. The contributions are not taxed again under any circumstances, as income taxes are paid before the funds are deposited in the account.

You can use the Roth IRA to maximum advantage by contributing assets that you expect will grow substantially in the period between deposit and withdrawal.

Life Insurance

Most people carry life insurance to cover their final expenses and to provide dependents with enough money to replace a portion of lost household income in case of death. The most common policies are term life programs, which means that they are effective for a certain period of time. Once the term is over, the policies have no value. Many employers offer staff members a term life policy as part of a comprehensive benefits package, and individuals can purchase private term life insurance through any carrier.

Term life insurance offers important protections, but it is not a method of increasing tax-free income to minimize tax liability. On the other hand, whole life insurance, also known as universal life insurance, is an entirely different sort of product. It still offers cash for final expenses and lost household income in case of your death, but unlike term insurance, this product builds value over time. A portion of your payments is invested, offering cash value that you can tap into if needed.

Whole life insurance is more expensive than term life policies, but the benefits last indefinitely, assuming you continue to pay the monthly premium. Many plans require payments for as long as the insurance is in force, but there are programs that offer finite payment schedules ranging from 10 – 25 years. Once you have completed the payment schedule, you continue to have the protection of life insurance as well as accessible cash value.

It is difficult to calculate the rate of return on the amount you invest in a whole life policy, but generally speaking, average earnings are comparable to standard savings and money market accounts. Because you pay your premiums with after-tax dollars, the cash value of your policy is tax-free if you choose to tap into it.

As an investment, whole life insurance is comparable to a Roth IRA, with added benefits for your dependents if you should die unexpectedly. You can use this product in conjunction with a Roth IRA to increase your tax-free income, because life insurance policies are not subject to income eligibility guidelines and contribution limits. It can also be a helpful solution for individuals who do not qualify for the Roth IRA program.

Annuities

Annuities have already been discussed as an option for deferring income tax, but they can also be an important component of a tax-free income strategy. As mentioned, contributions to some annuities can be made with pre-tax dollars, so income taxes are deferred until you begin receiving your annuity payments. However, many of the annuities available are set up to accept contributions made with after-tax dollars. As a result, a percentage of your future annuity payments are tax-free, which can be an extraordinarily effective way of reducing overall taxes.

There is a lot of flexibility in the terms of annuities, so it is possible to customize a plan based on your specific needs. For example, you can make payments into an annuity at regular intervals for a few years or a few decades, or you can choose to invest a single lump sum. If you come into a large amount of money all at once, for instance through an inheritance or lottery win, you may elect to purchase an annuity with a lump sum, which guarantees you a source of tax-free income for life.

Your annuity contract specifies how you will receive payments. For example, you may choose to receive a check once a month, once a quarter, or once a year when the payment period begins. The amount you receive is typically the same for each payment, and the amount is guaranteed for the agreed upon duration of payments. In most cases, payments will last for your lifetime, and often, annuities are set up to provide tax-free income for spouses or other dependents. Of course, the longer the payment period, the lower each payment will be.

Annuities are an attractive option for many, because there are no contribution limits for annuities as there are for other tax-deferred and tax-exempt products. There are also estate planning benefits to annuities, as these funds pass directly to your beneficiaries without the complications of probate. Furthermore, if you elect a guaranteed death benefit in your contract, your beneficiaries will receive a certain base payout, regardless of how your investments perform.

Transitioning to Tax-Free Income

As you are putting together a map to maneuver through the tax maze, you might discover that you made a wrong turn. Many people begin with tax-deferred accounts when they would be better served by tax-exempt accounts. For example, they make contributions to an employer-sponsored 401(k) to take advantage of the company's matching funds benefit, but after leaving the organization, it becomes clear that a tax-free income strategy offers a valuable opportunity to reduce tax liability long-term. Fortunately, it is easy to get back on the right path.

Rolling assets over from a tax-deferred retirement account to a tax-exempt Roth IRA account is referred to as a Conversion Roth IRA. At one time, income eligibility requirements applied to Conversion Roth IRAs just as they did with standard Roth IRAs, but that requirement is no longer in place as of 2010. As a result, you might hear a Conversion Roth IRA referred to as a "backdoor" Roth IRA, because those who are not otherwise eligible to participate in the program can obtain a Roth IRA through the Conversion method.

Your Certified Tax Coach is an excellent resource to guide you through the tax planning process, and it is important to engage that expertise. As you convert from tax-deferred to tax-free accounts, you must pay taxes on amounts that were not previously taxed. The sooner you can do this, the better, as the taxes you owe will increase with your earnings until the conversion is complete.

The Impact of Social Security on Your Tax-Free Income Strategy

No discussion of tax-free income strategies would be complete without a look at Social Security. While income from Social Security is partially tax-free, it must be considered as part of your larger income picture. The monthly amount you receive from Social Security adds to your total income, which can impact your tax rate for other income sources.

The most important thing you can do to maximize the value of your Social Security income is to wait as long as possible before starting to receive payments. Your lifetime monthly Social Security income is cal-culated based on when you start receiving distributions and your life expectancy, so the earlier you start receiving payments, the lower each check will be for as long as you live.

Many people elect to use funds from tax-deferred retirement plans and investment accounts at the start of their retirement, switching over to Social Security and Roth IRA distributions as other income sources are exhausted. Social Security and Roth IRA distributions work well to-gether, as withdrawals from your Roth IRA are tax-free.

Minimizing the tax you pay requires a careful, long-term strategy, and mapping out your success often includes a combination of tax re-duction tactics. Tax-free income opportunities are an important com-ponent of your plan, and you have a variety of options to choose from. Consider the benefits of some of the most preferred strategies. A Roth IRA allows you to earn tax-free income on your investments. Whole life insurance is another solid option to get you safely through the maze, because you make payments with after-tax dollars and cash value builds tax-free. Finally, you may wish to invest in an annuity, which can offer tax-free income for life.

Your Certified Tax Coach and professional financial planners offer the experience and expertise you need to get safely through the tax maze and make your investments work for you. These specialists ensure that the details of your situation are considered when creating your custom-ized tax planning strategy, so that you can look forward to a future of tax-free income.

ABOUT THE AUTHOR

Meryl B. Greenwald, CPA, CTC

Meryl Greenwald is a Certified Public Accountant, Certified Tax Coach, and owner of M. Greenwald Associates LLP, and has been saving clients' tax dollars since 1984. Her motto has always been, "Tax Day just records History. Plan for your future NOW!"

Ever since graduating from Ithaca College in 1983, Meryl knew taxes were going to be in her future. After graduation, she worked as an internal auditor for the Hertz Corporation which sent her traveling all over the United States and Canada. That is when she felt the pull toward taxes. So where do you go to learn more about taxes? The Internal Revenue Service. In her time working for the IRS, she learned all aspects of tax law and saw the inner workings of IRS Audits from individuals to corporations, since she did them all. Meryl was sought out by a CPA firm and left the IRS. After seven years working at the CPA firm, there was a stronger force pulling her; that force was her father and they teamed up and became M. Greenwald Associates LLP in 1994. They built their firm on the good knowledge and planning they provided to their clients.

Meryl loves to help all her clients save tax dollars just as much as she loves going to the theater and listening to music in small intimate settings. She enjoys spoiling her niece and nephews by spending quality time on a mini vacation with each of them.

Meryl can be reached at (201)863-5348 or at Meryl@MGAssociatesLLP.com. Visit her website at MGAssociatesLLP.com for newsletters and tax tips.

CHAPTER 4

The Journey Home: Saving Big on Deductions with Your Home-Based Business

BY LARISA HUMPHREY, EA, CTC, CTS

Starting a home-based business combines two dreams for many entrepreneurs: the advantages of working from home and the satisfaction of building a small business from the ground up. However, the tax maze gets even more complicated when you combine work and home, and there are important details to consider for long-term success. This is your guide to maximizing your profitability as you make your way through the home-based business maze.

First Steps: Getting Through Barriers to Entry

Running a home-based business comes with a variety of benefits, inspiring many to pursue this path. These businesses offer the flexibility of self-employment without the significant risk that most entrepreneurs face. Of course, lower risk comes with lower reward, and home-based businesses can take longer to become profitable as compared to more traditional businesses. Many entrepreneurs ease into self-employment by working another job until their company starts showing a profit that is large enough to live on. You can ensure that your transition from the corporate world to owning your own business goes smoothly by giving careful consideration to these questions:

- Do you have the right characteristics to successfully operate a home-based business?
- What type of business is right for you?
- Which regulations and tax laws will apply?

Answering these questions will help you identify any obstacles in your way so that you can plan ahead before entering the maze.

Characteristics of Successful Home-Based Business Owners

Evaluating your ability to operate a home-based business is important, but not in the way you might think. There are a lot of misconceptions when it comes to who can successfully balance the challenges of working from home. Some insist that only introverts can handle the isolation that comes with a home office, while others are convinced that only extroverts have what it takes to make connections with prospective customers. Perhaps the most common misconception is the widespread belief that productivity suffers when business owners don't have an office to go to each day.

In truth, it doesn't matter if you are an introvert or an extrovert, and going to an office has nothing to do with productivity. Studies have clearly demonstrated that extroverts thrive in a home-based environment because they have the skills necessary to make connections with people they come in contact with, whether through phone, video chat, or in-person meetings, minimizing feelings of isolation.

Introverts also surprised researchers with their ability to make virtual connections. For many introverts, removing the pressure of the constant interactions necessary in an office environment gave them more energy to successfully manage important relationships as needed.

Finally, business owners are generally able to balance the demands of their business with their family obligations while managing their companies from home. Most find that any interruptions during the workday are offset by the ability to put in a bit of extra time when it is more convenient schedule-wise, for example early mornings or after family members have gone to bed. The flexibility of adjusting work schedules to fit their lifestyles makes it easier to create balance, while still successfully managing their businesses.

The characteristics of a successful home-based business owner aren't about your personality type. In fact, they are quite broad. You must be adaptable and able to quickly adjust to changing circumstances, open to learning and applying new ideas and skills, and passionate about what you do. Getting any business off the ground is a marathon—not a sprint—and there will be some hard times. Your passion is the quality that will see you through. The best way to ensure that your passion stays strong is to build a home-based business that inspires you.

Building a Home-Based Business That Inspires You

Some types of businesses are known for being easy to adapt to a home environment, while others are typically operated in a traditional office setting or storefront. The rise of e-commerce has changed how consumers shop, and entrepreneurs have more options for home-based businesses than ever before. The first step in choosing the right home-based business is to consider what you are passionate about, where your experience lies, and which skills you already have.

You may know exactly what sort of business you want to run. For example, if you have been a successful real estate agent for many years, your plan might be to strike out on your own, operating an agency from your home. However, for many entrepreneurs, the choice isn't quite as clear. They know they want to work from home, but they aren't sure what sort of business fits their passion.

If you fall into the second group, don't worry. Countless books, magazines, and websites are devoted to this topic. Spend some time exploring the many at-home business opportunities available until you find something that matches your interests, abilities, and lifestyle. Think outside the box. Your primary skills and experience might be just right for a type of business that is in the same general industry—but not exactly the same job—as your previous employment.

Finally, don't feel obligated to start a unique business if you are less interested in the job itself and more interested in the work-from-home aspect. Many organizations are hiring home-based employees and independent contractors to provide customer service, technical support, and other kinds of assistance for their clients.

Avoid Get-Rich-Quick Scams

Unfortunately, there are scammers out there waiting to take advantage of new entrepreneurs by promising to provide all of the tools you need for lucrative home-based business, in exchange for some sort of fee. While these offers aren't always scams, the old adage certainly applies: if it sounds too good to be true, it probably is.

Before sending anyone your hard-earned money, do the same in-depth research you would with any other product or service. Check with consumer organizations like the Better Business Bureau, your state Attorney General's office, and the Federal Trade Commission's online consumer site. You can also use social media and review websites to your advantage. Many large groups and forums for entrepreneurs include feedback on current opportunities floating around.

Most important, don't give your personal information to anyone until you are absolutely certain that the organization is legitimate. Remember that scammers aren't always after your cash. For some, the payoff comes from collecting important details like your name, social security number, and so forth.

Buying an Existing Home-Based Business or Franchise

If your primary interest is in operating a home-based business and avoiding the stress that comes with building a company from the ground up, buying an existing business could be the right solution. The original owner has already laid the groundwork, so your initial role will be to transition infrastructure and current clients from the previous owner to you. The best practices that apply to buying any type of business apply to this situation as well, and there are additional factors to keep in mind.

The most important issue to explore before committing to a transaction is why the current owner is selling the business. For example, did he or she learn that such a business cannot legally be operated out of the home? Ask all of the same questions you would in a traditional sale, carefully examine financial records, and look at the existing client base, reputation, and competition.

If you aren't quite sure that buying someone else's business is right for you, but you like the idea of taking over a company that already has a foundation in place, joining a franchise might be the best choice. You pay a fee to enjoy instant name recognition and an existing reputation, and most franchises provide start-up kits, training, and long-term support. While you still own the business, a franchise offers you the opportunity to get some of the benefits that come with a large corporation. Of course, the trade-off is that you have to follow the franchise's rules. If you elect to go this route, make sure you work with a qualified attorney and your Certified Tax Coach to review the franchise agreement. These contracts can be fairly complicated, and it is critical to understand the detailed expectations you will have to meet under the contract's terms as well as the tax implications of becoming a franchise owner.

Choosing a Business Entity that Minimizes Liability and Taxes

When you own your own business, you typically start off as a sole proprietor until you take steps to create a separate business entity. As a sole proprietor, your personal finances and your business finances intermingle, and when the business operates from your home, things get even more intertwined. Many entrepreneurs are comfortable with sole proprietorships, but make sure you carefully research your options. The implications of choosing a business entity are too important to leave to chance.

There are two significant issues with sole proprietorships. First, unless you take action to incorporate, you can be held personally and financially responsible for your business activities and vice versa. That means that if a client sues your business, he or she may be able to access your personal assets. And if someone sues you—if you are liable for damages due to a car accident, for example—the individual filing suit against you may be able to seize your business assets. Legally, you and your business are the same entity when you operate a sole proprietorship.

The second issue with permitting your personal finances and your business finances to intermingle is tax ramifications. As a sole proprietor, you pay self-employment taxes in addition to income taxes. While this may make sense under certain circumstances, it is best to consult your Certified Tax Coach to be sure you have chosen the appropriate business entity and that you are taking advantage of all opportunities to minimize your tax expense.

The alternative to combining your personal and business affairs is to incorporate. Entities such as Limited Liability Companies (LLC) and S-Corporations exist completely separately from you. They take on their own liability and they are taxed under separate rules through your personal tax return.   Your personal assets are protected and the entity can continue to exist with its own life beyond its owner. The only caveat to this approach is that once you legally separate yourself from your home-based business, you must make it a point to keep the two separate. If you start intermingling funds or there is too much overlap between home life and work life, you may not be able to enjoy the benefits of incorporation and you may put yourself at risk for non-compliance with the tax code.

Next Steps: Operating Your Home-Based Business

Once you have made the important decisions as far as what type of business you want to own and how you want to structure it, the next step is to maneuver the maze of business regulations. All of the standard business rules apply, for example employment laws and tax requirements, and there can be additional regulations specific to home-based companies. Here are some of the most critical regulations to familiarize yourself with:

- **Zoning and Permitting** – Federal, state, and local regulations divide real estate into zones, for example, residential and commercial. These regulations place limits on the activities that can be performed within these zones. You are probably not allowed to run a retail store out of your garage, and you certainly can't live on the premises of a commercial warehouse. Review the zoning regulations for your area to determine whether the business you plan to operate from your home meets zoning requirements. You may have to apply for a permit to start certain kinds of home-based businesses, and you should be prepared to discover that some business types are completely prohibited.

- **Licensing** – There is a common misconception that you don't need a license to operate a business from your home, even if you would normally need a license to be employed in that profession. Common examples include accountants, massage therapists, and daycare providers. If you need a license to get a job in the industry, you need a license to practice from home, and your home itself may also need to be licensed or otherwise inspected. Make sure you have all appropriate licenses taken care of before you take your first client.

- **Federal, State, and Local Employment Laws** – If you have others working for you, it is important to be aware of federal, state, and local employment laws. While many are designed for companies with more than a handful of employees, there are a few that apply to every employee, no matter how small your company is. For example, the Fair Labor Standards Act which regulates minimum wage and child labor applies to everyone, whereas the Family and Medical Leave Act only applies to companies with fifty or more employees. Make sure you know which laws apply to you and make it a point to follow them carefully.

- **Copyright Infringements** – As you plan your products or services, give some thought to what you are providing. Can anyone else say that they own your images or ideas? Even though you are a small business, larger organizations will still protect their intellectual property fiercely. For example, if you are running a cleaning service, stay away from calling yourself Mr. Clean. Avoid using business names and taglines that could be confused with other companies' and take care to limit your products and services to ideas and images you own or have a legal right to use.

Ensuring Financial Security

No doubt you are familiar with the importance of insurance, and you probably already have policies on your home, car, and life. When you start a home-based business, spend some time with your financial advisor to discuss the special protections you will need as a business owner. Here are some of the most common policies small business owners purchase:

- **Health Insurance** – Going without health insurance is a serious gamble. One illness or accident can ruin you financially. Unfortunately, leaving your employer usually means leaving your health insurance behind as well. Carefully sort through your options for buying health insurance. You may be eligible for COBRA through your former employer or it might be possible to join your spouse's plan. Health insurance companies give you the opportunity to purchase individual policies, and in most states, you can access all of the choices online through a state-operated database.

- **Property Insurance** – Examine your existing homeowner's policy and speak with your agent about your current coverage. Often, business assets are excluded from residential homeowner's insurance. If this is the case for you, consider separate property insurance to cover business assets, as well as liability insurance to protect employees, customers, and suppliers. The same exclusions may apply to your personal auto insurance, so it is worth looking at that policy, as well.

- **Business Interruption and Disability Insurance** – If your home-based business is a significant source of household income, you will experience hardship if something happens to disrupt your business operations. A natural disaster or illness may temporarily prevent you from working, in which case you will need business interruption and/or disability insurance to replace lost income.

This list only covers insurance basics. There are a number of additional policies that may be sensible for your particular industry. Healthcare and professional services providers should have malpractice insurance. Employees of companies that enter people's homes, to make repairs or to clean for example, should be bonded against theft. If your company handles clients' money, you may need to ensure that employees are bonded against embezzlement. Finally, if you are selling a product you invented, product liability insurance will protect you and your company if something goes wrong. Your insurance agent, your attorney, and your financial advisor are excellent resources to assist in making these decisions.

Minimizing Tax Liability

You may have decided on a home-based business to save on the expense of renting office space. However, that isn't the only way to save money. Thanks to your home-based business, you may be eligible to claim deductions for certain expenses related to your home office. This is referred to as the home office tax deduction, and it applies to those who use a portion of their homes for business purposes. While calculating the correct deduction can be a challenge, your tax savings make the effort worthwhile, and your Certified Tax Coach can help. This has become even more critical under the new tax reform tax laws. With fewer deductions available for individual taxpayers through itemizing, business owners can deduct more by using the home office deduction.

You may be able to deduct a percentage of your utility bills, mortgage interest, depreciation, and repairs if you meet all of the following criteria established by the IRS:

- Your home office must be used exclusively for business.
- Your home office must be used regularly for business.
- Your home office must be your principle place of business or it must be used as a place for you to meet with clients for your business.

The requirement that your home office is used exclusively for business means that there must be a specific area in your home that isn't used for any other reason. You can't use this space for hobbies or family activities, and you can't use it for other business reasons if the other business doesn't meet the home office qualifications. Of course, there are some exceptions to this rule. For example, if you operate a home-based daycare, you can still qualify for this deduction even though the children are likely to spend time in multiple areas throughout your home.

The requirement that states that your home must be used regularly for business to qualify for a home office deduction means that you should be in that office for most of the time spent running your business. Those who do have a separate office in another facility and use their home office once or twice a week would not qualify. However, this won't be a problem if you are running a business that is entirely home-based. If you have any questions about whether your home office qualifies for a deduction, consult with your Certified Tax Coach.

Building a home-based business from the ground up or purchasing a successful home-based business and making it even better is an exciting way to get involved in the world of entrepreneurship. You can pursue your passion part time if you aren't ready to plunge in completely, and you have the convenience and flexibility of managing your business from home. Because you don't have to worry about all of the overhead expenses that come with acquiring and maintaining a separate property, your business may be more profitable more quickly, giving you a chance to build your wealth while doing something that you love. For many, this path through the financial maze combines the best of both worlds.

ABOUT THE AUTHOR
LARISA HUMPHREY, EA, CTC, CTS

I Paid More Taxes Than a Billionaire!

I started Abundant Returns Tax Service back in 1991 after seeing on TV that Ross Perot, then presidential candidate and CEO of a multibillion-dollar corporation, **paid less than $2,000 in personal income taxes!**

I just couldn't believe it because…

I made $35,000 that year and paid <u>More Than $4,000</u> in federal taxes alone!

I paid <u>*more than double*</u> the taxes a billionaire paid!

I was flabbergasted, to say the least.

"He is a billionaire," I kept saying to myself. "How is it legal for me to pay more taxes than a billionaire?"

I kept tossing it around in my head. I just couldn't believe it. I worried about how I was going to pay the rent. I struggled to buy a bus pass every week. I had to make "arrangements" every month to pay my utility bills. My grocery budget was $15/week and I was paying more income taxes than a billionaire?!!!

This was an "aha" moment for me—a life lesson that shattered my very sheltered view of reality. I learned two very valuable lessons: life is not fair and rich people can avoid income taxes.

So I got busy:

I took several income-tax-preparation courses.

I read hundreds of books on taxes. I prepared thousands of tax returns.

I worked for the IRS and a local tax office. I learned how to use tax law to my advantage. I learned how to live "tax-free"—like billionaires do.

Now I'm ready to share that knowledge with you so you can "**Keep More Money In Your Pocket**" too. In my ebook, "Pay Yourself Instead of Uncle Sam," I explore many tax strategies that will help you reduce your taxes as low as possible. You can find it at www.find-business-tax-deductions.com.

You can contact me at larisa@abundantreturns.com or feel free to give me a call at 770-451-6330.

CHAPTER 5

Expertly Navigating the Labyrinth of the Tax Code: 23 Tax Saving Tips for Doctors

BY THOMAS N. GEARHART, JR., CPA, CTC

Benjamin Franklin once said, "nothing can be said to be certain, except death and taxes." While this remains true today, physicians are in an excellent position to delay or minimize both. Because physicians add indispensable value to their communities, tax regulations offer them extra opportunities for tax savings. Some of the most common deductions include equipment, travel to conferences, and continuing education credits, but that is just the beginning. There are a wide variety of additional deductions available, particularly for physicians who own their practice. Your Certified Tax Coach is an excellent resource for assistance in locating thousands of dollars in tax savings.

Whether you are just starting out or you've been practicing for years, the tips below can boost your bottom line by allowing you to keep more of your earnings. You may not be able to implement all of these strategies at once but making small changes now can provide big financial benefits both short- and long-term.

Assemble an Advisory Team to Assist in Financial Planning

There are plenty of free and low-cost tools available to assist with tax planning but relying on these may cost you more in the long run. Internet programs and blog posts are either overly general to ensure one-size-fits-all, or they offer information on detailed scenarios that may or may not apply to you. Gathering a team of expert financial advisors, including an experienced accountant and a Certified Tax Coach, will ensure that your strategy is customized to your unique needs.

Choose financial professionals with the specialized knowledge required to advise healthcare providers. This saves you time and money in the long run, as they already understand the nuances of your continuing education expenses, how your costly medical equipment should be depreciated, and so on. Your team should include a retirement planning specialist who understands the challenges of operating a successful medical practice, as well as a debt specialist with deep knowledge on the ins and outs of student loans. These two factors weigh heavily on your ability to successfully start a business and to save for long-term goals like retirement.

Once you have enlisted the support of highly qualified financial service providers, be sure to meet with them regularly. For example, Certified Tax Coaches add the most value when you review significant expenses with them before making an investment rather than afterward. Slight variables impact whether costs can be deducted from your taxable income. Understanding how to spend your money wisely is just as important as saving it.

Finding time for face-to-face meetings while you're trying to run a medical practice might seem impossible, but it pays off, and you can always take advantage of videoconference technology in a pinch. New tax saving opportunities arise all the time, so keeping communication open throughout the year is key to getting the most out of your financial advisory team.

Remember, a quick appointment during tax filing season won't suffice. This is the busiest time of year for most financial services professionals, and they simply don't have capacity for an in-depth analysis of your strategy during this period. However, by staying in touch throughout the year, you can count on minimizing your tax liability when it is time to file your returns.

Keep in mind that the final decision on any matter regarding your finances belongs to you. Though your team is there to provide information and guidance, you will have to live with the choices you make. Ensure you are comfortable with the strategies you select and eliminate any members of your team who use high-pressure sales tactics. Stay on top of new developments in tax regulations, and do some independent research on investing, retirement planning, and debt reduction techniques. This will allow you to lead your financial advisory team, rather than relying on them to lead you.

Contribute to Your Retirement Account

Make it a habit to contribute the maximum amount allowed to your retirement account. From a long-term perspective, it's never too early to get serious about retirement. The sooner you start saving, the more you will benefit from the magic of compound interest. Short-term, you may enjoy immediate tax savings, as it is often possible to deduct a percentage of your retirement contributions from your taxable income.

Setting a portion of your income aside for retirement can be especially difficult if you are starting your own practice—all the more so if you have student loans to pay back. Don't be discouraged if you can only afford small contributions at first. The sooner you begin to put money into your retirement account, the faster your investment will grow. Time is a critical factor in the final value of your investments, which is why it's best to start saving early.

Timing the Market

Anyone who has considered investing in products other than standard checking, savings, money markets, and CDs knows this basic rule: buy low, sell high. Unfortunately, that is far easier said than done. Financial markets move in cycles, and even the most experienced market analysts admit that they can't predict when highs and lows will occur. For the purpose of building wealth, making regular contributions to your accounts over time is the most reliable way to be sure your portfolio grows.

Consider Investments That Minimize Tax Liability

In today's marketplace, you can invest money in everything imaginable. For example, some mutual funds focus on traditional energy sources, while others exclusively invest in green initiatives. You can purchase stock in individual companies whether they are headquartered in the United States or somewhere else in the world, and you can invest in specific commodities such as metals, agricultural products, and livestock. Of course, any time you make money on an investment, you can be sure there is a relevant tax regulation. Understanding your options—and how different types of earnings will be taxed—should be a consideration as you design your investment strategy.

The wide variety of mutual funds offers an excellent example of products with varying tax liability. Some mutual funds are specifically designed to maximize dividends. This is helpful for investors who want regular income that will be taxed at the capital gains rate. However, if your goal is minimizing your current tax liability, such investments may not be right for you.

Dividends will increase your taxable income, perhaps to the point of pushing you into a higher tax bracket. Instead, you may wish to consider a mutual fund that is centered around a long-term capital gains strategy. Better still, you could invest in tax-free government or municipal bonds, which are exempt from federal income tax. In some cases, there is no state or municipal tax liability on these earnings.

Investors intending to keep tax liability low generally choose a buy-and-hold strategy rather than interest or dividend paying products. If minimizing your taxes is high on your list of financial priorities, these types of investments could be right for you. More information on specific funds, stocks, and bonds are available through your financial services providers or from sources such as Morningstar, The Wall Street Journal, Kiplinger's Personal Finance, and SmartMoney.

Prioritize Record-Keeping

As a physician, you already know the importance of record-keeping. Your patients rely on you to keep their files up-to-date, with every detail carefully documented. The same goes for your financial affairs. It is far too easy to forget expenses over the course of a year—particularly the small ones. These can add up to large deductions when combined on your tax return.

Tax rules change during the year, so having proof of when you made a purchase may lower your tax bill. For example, the 2003 Tax Act adjusted the bonus depreciation percentage from 30 percent to 50 percent for qualified property. However, this benefit only applied to property acquired after May 5, 2003, and before January 1, 2005. Without receipts and detailed notes, it can be difficult to validate that assets were purchased during the appropriate time period.

You can be required to produce verification of the information included in your returns at any time. Your notes and receipts are crucial here. If you have incorporated your business, minutes of your meetings may also be needed to validate items on your tax returns. Without careful documentation, you may be unable answer questions from the IRS if you are ever audited. This gets expensive—and if the IRS determines that you owe back taxes, you could be liable for interest and penalties on top of the actual tax payments.

When documenting expenses for tax purposes, each entry should include the amount of the expense as well as the date, time, and place of the purchase. Be sure to note whether and how the expenditure is related to your business and save each receipt as backup.

While many physicians keep their receipts in a shoebox, you may wish to invest in software that is specifically designed to assist you in tax-related record-keeping. Digital copies of your paperwork are easier to manage than the hard copies, though hard copies can be retained as backup. Check with your Certified Tax Coach for a software recommendation, as it is far easier to send your notes over when you and your financial advisors are working with the same programs.

Finally, take advantage of available technology to simplify your record-keeping. The same voice recorders you use to document patients' visits can be used to record expense-related reminders, ensuring that you can take advantage of every deduction you are entitled to. A variety of mobile apps have been developed to record items like business-related mileage, meals, and entertainment. Choose your favorite technology and use it to track items that might otherwise slip through the cracks.

Create a Business Entity that Works for You

Building a thriving private practice is the number one goal for many healthcare providers. Unfortunately, even the busiest practices aren't always financially successful. The design of your business can be just as important as how many patients you see when it comes to long-term profits.

Your final tax bill is strongly influenced by the type of business entity you select: Sole Proprietorship, Partnership, Corporation, or Limited Liability Company. There are pros and cons to each option. For example, a Sole Proprietorship gives you 100 percent control over business decisions. The profits from your practice are reported as a part of your personal income, and typically, estimated taxes are not withheld or paid throughout the year. Sole proprietorships and Partnerships including LLC's are subject to self-employment tax, while S corporation earnings are not. However, under the new tax reform laws, personal service companies like medical practices may not benefit from being a Sole Proprietorship, S Corporation or Partnership.

On the other hand, a Corporation is completely separate from you for tax purposes. Under the tax reform laws, the C corporate flat tax rate of 21%—even for personal service companies—is mighty attractive as well. Decision-making may be shared among everyone who owns a portion of the company, and taxes are assessed to the business instead of to you as an individual. Depending on your circumstances, this could be a less expensive option for your practice. Your advisory team will offer advice on the best way to set up your practice for insurance and liability purposes, and your Certified Tax Coach is available to guide you on the tax ramifications of your choice.

Consider Creative Options to Save on Taxes

Physicians who own their business are often able to use a collection of tax-minimization strategies that are not available to healthcare providers employed by others. Leverage the experience and expertise of your financial advisory team to ensure you take advantage of every available opportunity. For example, one creative and effective method of lowering your tax liability is putting your children on the payroll. Of course, they must be performing legitimate, age-appropriate work in exchange for their wages. By enlisting your children to take on tasks like filing, appointment reminder calls, and other housekeeping activities, your business gets a tax deduction. Meanwhile, neither your children nor your household will be assessed taxes for their income, as long as it falls under the specified threshold. Note that these particular benefits only apply to children who are your dependents and are under the age of eighteen.

Another unusual and effective option is to create a closely held insurance company. Such companies can be helpful in the event of revenue drops, file losses, or lawsuits, and you gain a variety of tax advantages. Speak with your Certified Tax Coach to determine whether this option is appropriate for you.

Decide Whether Deferring Compensation Makes Sense

Your tax bracket has a significant impact on the total amount of taxes you pay, and the progression is anything but gradual. If you experienced a sudden, temporary increase in your income, you may discover that a large portion is lost to taxes. In this situation, you may be able to defer some compensation. Essentially, part of the compensation you earn this year is set aside and paid out at a later date. In many cases, deferred compensation is earmarked for retirement. The immediate benefit is that you generally will not pay taxes on deferred compensation in the year that you earn it. When you receive the lump sum upon retirement, your tax liability may be lower. Your Certified Tax Coach is the best resource for more information on whether deferring a portion of your compensation is the right decision to minimize your taxes. Many healthcare providers are also using deferred compensation as a way to reduce taxable income in order to qualify for a new tax deduction allowed under tax reform.

Take Advantage of Available Deductions

Sometimes, a minor change in how you operate your business can result in significant tax savings. By taking a different path to achieve specific outcomes, you gain eligibility for additional deductions. These are just a few examples of potential tax-saving techniques:

Owning vs. Leasing – You can depreciate medical equipment that you purchase for your practice, but that isn't always the path to greatest tax savings. In some cases, leasing is a better option, as you may be able to deduct the full expense.

Volunteer Work – The essence of volunteering your time is the fact that it is an unpaid contribution to your community, but that doesn't mean you have to shoulder the entire burden of expenses you incur along the way. If you are providing free services and using equipment you purchased to do so, the expense of the equipment may be deductible. You can also take a charitable deduction for mileage related to travelling to and from the volunteer site. Of course, as with any other expenses, keep records to support any deductions listed on your returns.

Employee Benefits – When you operate a small practice, the cost of employee benefits can appear overwhelming—particularly if you are just starting out. However, you may reconsider your position once you gain an understanding of the tax deductions available to you for these expenses. Regulations are designed to encourage you to provide retirement savings and health insurance, which means you may qualify for reduced tax rates when you offer these to your staff members.

Home Offices – Most physicians have space in their home specifically dedicated to business-related activities. In some cases, entire rooms are set aside to see patients. When handled according to very specific requirements, you can deduct a portion of your home expenses to account for this income-producing space.

Income-Producing Pastimes – Everyone needs a way to unwind. For some, playing with a band on the weekends is a creative outlet, while others practice another form of artistic expression. If any of your creative hobbies turn into a source of income, be sure to make it official. Turning your side project into a small business gives you many of the same tax-minimization options you use for your medical practice.

Note that this also applies to activities that are separate from your practice but still related to your profession. If you earn income through writing, teaching, or providing expert testimony, you may wish to secure these earnings under the title of another small business.

Finally, if you aren't sure whether an expense can be deducted, go ahead and log it in your records. Your Certified Tax Coach can help you sort through all of your receipts. Don't risk missing out on any tax savings because you aren't quite sure whether certain expenses are eligible.

Learn More About State and Local Tax Laws

Federal taxes take the biggest bite from your budget, but state and local taxes should not be ignored. These add up to a substantial amount if you neglect relevant tax minimization strategies. Your state and municipal lawmakers are responsible for local tax code, and they are tasked with raising money for major projects. They may also use tax-related legislation to encourage or discourage particular behavior. For example, physicians may enjoy lower taxes if they choose to operate in a distressed or underserved community. Increase your awareness of local tax regulations that apply to your practice and consider incorporating them into your overall tax minimization planning.

In conclusion, a comprehensive wealth-building strategy requires that you dedicate effort and attention to both your short-term and your long-term savings and investing tactics. Careful day-to-day record-keeping ensures your taxes stay low in the short-term, while developing sound saving, investing, and financial management habits puts you in an excellent position to reach your long-term objectives. Decisions you make now have a lasting impact, whether it is how you structure your business or the amount you contribute to retirement savings each year. Consult your Certified Tax Coach regularly to keep yourself on track for success.

ABOUT THE AUTHOR

Thomas N. Gearhart, Jr., CPA, CGMA, CTC, FACMPE

Thomas N. Gearhart, Jr., is a busy Managing Director at TNgearhart Company, a healthcare consulting firm, and President of Kozleski CPAs. Previously, he was CEO for an Illinois private orthopedic medical practice. Mr. Gearhart was CEO of Close Scrutiny, Inc., an international consulting firm established to help other accountants understand healthcare metrics and strategic planning facilitation techniques. Mr. Gearhart was managing partner at DLMG Accountants+Advisors, a regional CPA firm headquartered in Colorado Springs, Colorado, and was instrumental in the firm's Healthcare Consulting Division. He works closely with other healthcare consultants around the nation to assist in providing quality services to physicians, medical groups, hospitals, and other organizations as they develop strategies for sound management for the future. Thom has published articles in regional publications and is frequently asked to speak on a variety of healthcare topics including decision support system development, physician and hospital affiliations, practice operations, and strategic planning. He is a Fellow in the American College of Medical Practice Executives and is a member of the Medical Group Management Association, American Institute of CPAs, and the Colorado Society of CPA's. He holds active CPA licenses in Colorado and Illinois, and is a Chartered Global Management Accountant and Certified Tax Coach. Thom graduated from Brigham Young University with a Bachelor's Degree in Accounting. During his thirty-five plus years in accounting and consulting, Thom has focused on helping organizations and individuals achieve their financial and business objectives.

Recently, while physician owners focused on providing world class orthopedic care to their patients, Mr. Gearhart's efforts yielded a phenomenal increase in capital value of the practice based on ever improving business results including:

- Recruitment of fourteen additional physicians, three new PA's, and thirty-one rehab therapists (PT, O/T, ATC) to the practice.
- Development of four new satellite operations.
- Developed relationships with hospital CEO's resulting in the addition of three new hospital system affiliations and unique service collaboration agreements.
- Developed tax strategies that decreased physician personal tax rates.
- Development of three new service lines and four centers of excellence.
- Increased transaction count 145% and collected revenue 165%.

CHAPTER 6

Finding the Right Route: Special Topics for LGBT Couples

BY DOMINIQUE MOLINA, CPA, CTS

The road to legalized marriage for same-sex couples has taken a lot of twists and turns. With every new piece of legislation and court decision, there have been changes in how tax returns should be filed. Some of the biggest questions have been around the application of tax benefits available to married LGBT couples. In fact, it was a tax question that led to one of the US Supreme Court's landmark rulings. Now that a national policy is in place, most of the outstanding tax issues have been resolved, and married LGBT couples can get reliable, consistent advice on keeping tax liability low. Your Certified Tax Coach has the experience and expertise needed to guide you through the complex tax maze so that you can save as much as possible.

A Brief History of Legislation Impacting Taxes for Married LGBT Couples

The passage of The Defense of Marriage Act (DOMA) in September 1996 made a blanket statement that for the purpose of federal benefits, the only marriages that would be recognized were those that existed between one man and one woman. As a result, same-sex couples who were legally married in states that recognized same-sex marriages could not benefit from insurance benefits for spouses of government employees, social security survivor benefits, and the filing of joint tax returns.

In 2013, the US Supreme Court declared that section of DOMA unconstitutional as a result of the case United States v. Windsor, which was originally around estate taxes. The same-sex surviving spouse of an individual who died was required to pay significantly more estate taxes than she would have if her marriage—legally performed in Canada—was recognized by the federal government.

At the time, the country was divided in its handling of same-sex marriages. Some states permitted these unions while others prohibited them. After the United States v. Windsor decision was announced, state and federal agencies scrambled to determine whether and how their existing policies and procedures would need to be adjusted to accommodate the change. In the meantime, financial planners and tax advisors had a lot of questions to be answered for themselves and their clients. For example, which federal benefits applied to couples who lived in a state where their marriage was recognized? Would federal benefits apply to couples who were legally married in a state where their marriage was recognized, but lived in a state where it was not recognized?

One of the most anticipated set of guidelines was finally issued by the IRS through Revenue Ruling 2013-17, the result of the Windsor case, which stated that all couples who were legally married would be eligible for related tax benefits, regardless of where they lived. Married same-sex couples were required to file their tax returns as married, and they could participate in programs designed to minimize taxes for surviving spouses when the other dies.

The landmark US Supreme Court case Obergefell v. Hodges (2015) was a victory for LGBT couples, giving them all of the same rights and responsibilities that come with marriage. This decision removed any uncertainty about whether and where marriages would be recognized. As a result of Obergefell v. Hodges, married same-sex couples can enjoy the same tax treatment as married opposite-sex couples, and they can benefit from financial planning designed to minimize taxes.

Federal Income Tax Planning for Married LGBT Couples

The 2013 Supreme Court decision meant that when same-sex married couples filed their 2013 returns, they were required to file using either the married filing single or married filing jointly status. The decision applied retroactively, so many couples elected to amend some or all of their returns for the previous three years to take advantage of additional tax savings. A statute of limitations applies to filing amended returns, so it wasn't possible to go back any further.

If you have been married, but you have not filed as married for any of the past three years, there is still time to review and correct your returns. The deadline for amending tax returns is either three years from the filing due date or two years from the date taxes were paid, whichever is later. The impact on your tax liability depends on several factors, but generally, your taxes will go down if income is disproportionally earned by one spouse, and they will go up if you earn roughly the same income.

The phenomenon of paying more taxes as a married couple than you would as two single taxpayers is referred to as "the marriage penalty." It happens because the tax bracket for higher-income married couples is higher than the tax bracket for higher-income single people. Once you are married, you have to make a decision about which filing status will benefit you most, married filing jointly or married filing single. Your Certified Tax Coach can help by determining your tax liability under each scenario.

The most important thing to understand is that as the combined income of you and your spouse increases, you are likely to pay more in taxes overall. This happens because there are dramatic differences between the single and married tax brackets as levels of income go up. It works like this:

For 2017, single taxpayers are in the 15 percent tax bracket up to a maximum taxable income of $37,950. Married couples stay in the 15 percent tax bracket up to a maximum taxable income of $75,900. You will notice that the married income ceiling is double that of the single income ceiling. However, as income levels increase, it isn't quite so cut and dry.

In 2017, single taxpayers stay in a 25 percent tax bracket up to a maximum income of $91,900. However, couples who are married filing jointly can only stay in the 25 percent tax bracket up to a maximum combined income of $153,100. As you can see, this is less than double the income rate of a single taxpayer. Essentially, married taxpayers who make a combined total of up to $153,100 pay more on their higher income levels than their peers who are single.

There are a number of reasons for the marriage tax penalty, and occasionally, laws are passed in an effort to ease the burden on married couples who are impacted by extra taxes. However, a significant revision of the tax code would be necessary to eliminate this penalty altogether.

IRS Requirements for Filing Your Returns as a Married Couple

Avoiding common errors on your tax returns will save the time and expense of amending and refiling your documents. If you are new to filing tax returns as a married couple, there are a few important points to be aware of:

- Married taxpayers must file as either married filing jointly or married filing single. Neither can use the head of household filing status, and spouses cannot be claimed as dependents.

- There is an exception to the rule above. Married couples who have lived apart for the last six months of the tax year can be considered unmarried for tax purposes. The individual responsible for providing more than half the cost of maintaining a household that includes his or her dependent child for at least those six months can choose the head of household filing status.

- Just one of the same-sex spouses who elect the married filing single status can claim each qualifying child as a dependent. If you both claim the same child, the IRS will adjust your tax returns. Generally, the deduction goes to the parent with whom the child lived for more than half the year. If the amount of time is equal, the deduction goes to the parent with higher adjusted gross income.

- Married couples must use the same option when it comes to itemizing deductions versus claiming the standard deduction.

- Employer-sponsored health insurance premiums are paid on a pre-tax basis. However, before the 2013 tax rules were released, the premiums for same-sex spouses were paid on an after-tax basis. If you discover that your premiums were taxed during a year that is still eligible for amendment, you can file an amended return to receive a refund for those taxes.

- If, as a sole proprietor, you employed your same-sex spouse, you might have overpaid FUTA taxes. If this occurred during a year that is still eligible for amendment, you can file an amended return to receive a refund for those taxes.

- As a reminder, the deadline for amending tax returns is either three years from the filing due date or two years from the date taxes were paid, whichever is later.

Note that these rights do not extend to legal domestic partnerships or civil unions for same-sex or opposite-sex couples on a federal level, though state tax laws may be different. It is also important to consider that some states automatically converted civil unions and domestic partnerships between LGBT couples to marriages after the 2015 Supreme Court decision. Together with your financial and tax professionals, look into the laws of your state to determine your status before filing your returns.

More Federal Tax Benefits for Married Couples

In addition to income tax requirements, married couples are given special treatment under a number of other federal tax laws. However, you must plan ahead to take full advantage of all available tax benefits and minimize your tax liability. Your Certified Tax Coach is an important resource when it comes to protecting your wealth, as these specialists have a deep understanding of the various regulations that could impact you. CTCs are also focused on long-term tax planning rather than individual annual returns.

Planning for Estate Taxes

Couples with large estates are impacted most by estate tax regulations, as each person can pass up to $11.2 million to beneficiaries without incurring taxes in 2018. For couples, careful planning can shield over $22 million from taxation. Estate tax regulations are particularly favorable to the surviving spouse of a person who has died. When you pass away, you can transfer your entire estate to your spouse, regardless of its size, without incurring estate taxes. Alternatively, you can leave part of your estate to your spouse and part of it to other beneficiaries. The inheritance for non-spouses will be tax-free up to the $5.49 million limit.

Couples that make the decision to transfer all assets from a first spouse to a second spouse do not have to give up the first individual's $11.2 million exemption. A feature known as portability allows the second spouse to use any remaining portion of the first spouse's exemption. However, there is an important caveat. If surviving spouses want to retain access to carryover exemptions from the person who pre-deceased them, the portability option must be selected on the first spouse's estate tax return.

As you might remember, United States v. Windsor was originally filed to prevent the federal government from barring same-sex married couples from taking advantage of these benefits. Now that the issue of whether married LGBT couples are eligible for these tax exemptions has been decided, make sure that your estate plan takes these regulations into consideration. Decisions you make now can significantly impact the amount of taxes your estate pays before your remaining wealth passes on to your spouse and other beneficiaries.

Minimizing Gift Taxes

Giving gifts to friends and family members is an opportunity to support loved ones as they make major purchases or move through significant life events, such as marriage, having a child, buying a home, or paying for their education. However, tax regulations limit the dollar amount of tax-free gifts you can make. For 2018, you can give as many individual gifts of up to $15,000 to anyone you wish without worrying about tax implications.

Married couples do not have to worry about gift exclusion limits for gifts made to each other. Tax regulations permit unlimited gifts between spouses without incurring additional taxes. In addition, each person can gift up to the exclusion limit to the same recipient. For example, in 2018 both spouses can gift up to $15,000 to the same child, totaling $30,000, without paying gift taxes. As a result of the 2013 IRS policy, these exceptions apply to legally married same-sex couples, and of course, the 2015 Supreme Court decision made same-sex marriage legal nationwide.

Maximizing Qualified Retirement Plan Benefits

Effective in 2013, all qualified retirement plans were required to recognize the legal marriage of same-sex couples, granting same-sex spouses all of the same privileges as opposite-sex spouses of qualified retirement plan participants. For example, spouses are the automatic beneficiaries of qualified retirement plans when the participant dies. Note that these rights do not extend to legal domestic partnerships or civil unions for same-sex or opposite-sex couples.

Your qualified retirement plan may give your spouse certain rights when it comes to what you can do with your savings. For example, you may need your spouse's permission to change your beneficiaries, take a loan, or make a withdrawal. The Summary Plan Description for your account offers additional details on these rules.

Calculating Taxes on Capital Gains and Losses when Married

When you sell any of your assets, the goal is usually to make a profit, and you will be required to pay capital gains taxes on that profit. However, there are many situations in which that simply doesn't happen, so you can avoid being taxed altogether. For example, you may have purchased your home at the height of the market, and now you need to relocate, or your business might have taken a nosedive. Fortunately, married couples get a little extra relief when it comes to calculating tax liability for capital gains and losses. Depending on the situation, you may be able to deduct your capital losses up to the amount of your capital gains plus $3,000. This figure is $1,500 for individuals who are married but filing separately. If your capital losses exceed the limit this year, you might be able to carry losses over to future years. It is important to note that if you sell assets to a family member at a loss, you cannot deduct capital losses.

Marriage makes it easier to avoid taxes on capital gains that result from the sale of your primary residence through the Home Sale Gain Exclusion Credit. If you sell a home that you owned and occupied as your principal residence for any two of the previous five years, up to $500,000 of married couples' capital gains may be excluded from capital gains taxes.

Taking Advantage of Education Credits

If you aren't in school but your spouse is, you may be able to apply for a Lifetime Learning Credit. You can receive up to a $2,000 tax credit to pay for qualified tuition and fees at eligible educational facilities. The primary factor in whether or not you are eligible to claim this benefit is your modified adjusted gross income (MAGI). For married couples who are filing jointly, the maximum income you can have and still qualify is $130,000.

It is also possible that you or your spouse could qualify for the American Opportunity Tax Credit. This program is specifically for individuals who are working through their first four years of college at a qualified institution, and you or your spouse may be eligible to receive a tax credit of up to $2,500. The income limits for the American Opportunity Tax Credit are a bit higher. You can qualify for the full amount if you are married, filing jointly, and have a MAGI of $132,000 or less. Partial amounts for MAGIs under $132,000 but above $112,000 may also be awarded.

Your Certified Tax Coach can help you determine whether you and your spouse should claim an education credit, and if so, which one. You cannot claim both on the same return for the same student.

Managing Business Taxes

When you and your spouse open a business, one of the most important decisions you will make is the type of business entity to create. Tax liability is calculated quite differently between Sole Proprietorships, Partnerships, LLCs, C-Corps, and S-Corps. In an effort to encourage the growth of small businesses, a 2007 law made it possible for married couples to operate joint ventures without declaring a formal partnership.

The Small Business and Work Opportunity Tax Act of 2007 states that married couples may enter into a qualified joint venture instead of a partnership, provided that the only members of the joint venture are the two spouses. Both spouses must agree on operating as a qualified joint venture, and both must be active participants in the business. This makes a difference in how business transactions are made, who owns which property (if applicable), and how taxes are calculated.

In partnerships, the business is a single entity, and the individual partners cannot act alone. All assets are owned by the partnership, and profits and losses are divided evenly. Joint ventures are a bit different. Each spouse retains his or her identity as an individual participant in the business, and each retains ownership of specific assets brought into the business.

For tax purposes, partnerships are treated much like sole proprietorships. Profits and losses pass through the business to the owners, who then declare the income or loss on their personal tax returns. Joint ventures offer owners another option. While they can still be taxed as a partnership if they meet certain qualifications, they can also be taxed as a corporation. This makes it unnecessary to report income and losses on your personal tax return. Your Certified Tax Coach can review these options with you to determine which tax method will benefit you and your spouse most.

Overall, the tax benefits of legal marriage for LGBT couples far outweigh the costs. However, realizing all of the tax benefits available requires a comprehensive strategy. Consult your Certified Tax Coach for more information on whether you should submit your returns under the status of married filing jointly or married filing single. You should also review estate planning strategies and options for gift giving that bring your overall tax liability down. Finally, take a look at tax credits you might not otherwise have claimed. As aforementioned, the Home Sale Gain Exclusion Credit, the Lifetime Learning Credit, and the American Opportunity Tax Credit may be an option for you or your spouse. You are entitled to all of the tax benefits that opposite-sex married couples have enjoyed for decades, and a comprehensive tax minimization strategy will ensure that you make it through the tax maze with your wealth intact.

ABOUT THE AUTHOR

Dominique Molina, CPA, CTS

Dominique Molina is the President and Founder of the American Institute of Certified Tax Planners. With over 15 years of experience as a Certified Public Accountant (CPA), Molina has worked with many top business owners and investors using proactive tax planning to help them keep more of what they earn. Molina is an accomplished key note speaker, teacher, best-selling author, and mentor to tax professionals across the United States. Molina began teaching and writing books to make individuals and tax professionals aware of government tax breaks and loopholes that most tax professionals miss. She is best known as the co-author of five best-selling books, most notably *Tax Breaks of the Rich and Famous* and *Secrets of a Tax Free Life*. She frequently appears in print, television, and radio programs, including CNN Money and is the host of the popular podcast, Business $ense, a weekly program for business owners and investors. Molina was named one of the 40 Most Influential Accountants by CPA Practice Advisor Magazine and a recipient of the 2014 Financial Services Champion Award from the SBA.

CHAPTER 7

Pursuing the Right Path: Which Business Entity is Right for You?

BY DALE HAMMERNIK, EA, ATA, CTC

Maneuvering through the intricacies of complex tax regulations isn't easy, but smart decisions early on can result in significant tax savings for years to come. One of the most important forks in the path is at the very beginning of the tax maze: deciding which business entity is best for your company. Examine the pros and cons of each, and consult with your Certified Tax Coach to choose the business entity that will maximize your wealth by minimizing your tax liability. This has never been more true than through the recent tax reform legislation.

Boosting Your Wealth Through Business Ownership

Many of the most successful people in the world give one piece of advice: no one becomes truly wealthy by working for others. These individuals make their fortunes by starting their own companies, producing products and services while taking advantage of the many tax incentives designed for business owners. The added ability to control their own destinies by running operations of their own businesses and managing their own finances is what results in their tremendous success.

When it comes to building wealth, the primary difference between business owners and employees relates to the options available for building a fortune. Flexibility is important, as successful investment requires good timing, access to resources, and diversification. Salaried employees are limited to two basic methods of saving and investing: they can move up the career ladder to earn more, or they can spend less. Business owners have these same options, but within them, there is a wide array of opportunity.

Business owners have an entire company to work with when it comes to increasing income, and a change in strategy can dramatically transform the bottom line. Profits go up when expenses come down, and business owners have significant control over costs. More importantly, business income is taxed differently than personal income, and in many cases, more favorably. By focusing on tax-reduction strategies, business owners can keep more of the money they generate.

The Impact of Choosing the Right Business Entity

Successful navigation of the tax maze means understanding the nuances of tax regulations. One of the most critical decisions that you will make is choosing the best structure for the type of business you will operate. For tax purposes, the legal structure of your business falls under a specific business entity. This is important, because the business entity affects how the business is taxed. For legal purposes, businesses are considered to be a separate taxpayer from their owner(s), with unique tax identification numbers and differentiated income and tax calculations.

There are benefits to this method of viewing businesses. For instance, under certain business entities, owners are not liable for business debts. This encourages innovation and risk-taking, as entrepreneurs can test out an idea without personally bankrupting themselves. Because of their status as unique legal entities, most businesses continue to exist even when their founder is no longer involved with the company. As a result, businesses can continue to operate when the owner sells the company, retires, or dies.

This status makes it possible for businesses to obtain credit as entities separate from their owners, and there is some continuity for employees and those who depend on the company, regardless of changes in leadership. Each type of business entity has pros and cons from a tax perspective, as the regulations for each vary. In some cases, the differences are enormous, while in others, they are quite nuanced. In all cases, individuals operating the same type of business with similar strategies and sales can see a wide variation in tax expenses depending on their choice of business entity during the original structure of the organization.

Consider this example:

John owns and operates a cleaning company as a sole proprietorship. His total profits are $50,000 per year. Because he is a sole proprietor, he is taxed at self-employment rates on 100 percent of the cleaning company's profits. At a rate of 15 percent, John's total tax liability is $7,500.

On the other hand, Maria owns and operates a cleaning company as an S-corporation. She pays herself a salary from the business, and she is able to take a distribution of the remaining profits as a separate transaction. If Maria pays herself a reasonable salary of $25,000 per year and takes distribution of the remaining $25,000, she is only required to pay self-employment tax on the $25,000. Taxes on the remaining $25,000 are considered under separate—and often more favorable—regulations.

Sole proprietorship is perhaps the easiest of business entities to set up, but it is often the most expensive. With a bit of guidance from the right Certified Tax Coach, you can easily find your way through the tax maze to select a better business entity, saving money on your taxes every year.

Finding Your Way to the Right Business Entity

Your choice of business entity will determine how your company's profits are taxed as well as your personal liability for business debts. The expertise of your attorney, accountant and Certified Tax Coach will be invaluable in getting you on the right path. Together with your team, you will consider the pros and cons of the six business entities that follow before you settle on the right choice for you and your business.

Sole Proprietorship

Most people who own and operate a business alone land on the sole proprietorship business entity by default. It is the easiest to set up, requiring little or no paperwork to start doing business. Individuals who operate under a business name other than their own legal name simply register their business name with the appropriate government agency. It appears as YOUR NAME DBA (Doing Business As) COMPANY NAME.

Sole proprietors must obtain appropriate licenses and certifications as required by local and state officials. The specific requirements depend on the type of business. For example, food service companies must have food handling licenses and food safety certifications. These are across-the-board regulations, regardless of the type of food service business.

Other than fulfilling these small requirements, anyone can start a sole proprietorship at any time. For legal and tax purposes, the individual and the business are the same, and income from sole proprietorship is taxed through the individual operating the business as regular income.

A sole proprietor can hire employees, but he retains sole ownership of his business. From a tax perspective, all business profits are treated as personal income, and sole proprietorship taxes are filed on the owner's personal tax return. The business owner is also personally liable for the company's debts as well as any litigation raised against the business.

In other words, if you're a freelance journalist working as a sole proprietor, you can be personally sued for libel for the things you write; if you're a journalist working for a company, the company itself is liable. There are exceptions to this, and the applicable laws can vary, so consult with an attorney if such issues arise.

Aside from their ease of creation, sole proprietorships offer few tax benefits. Sole proprietors tend to pay more in taxes than other types of business owners because 100 percent of the company's profits are subject to both income and self-employment taxes.

Pros:

- A sole proprietorship is the simplest business to set up.
- You will have minimal operating costs.

- There are few startup and administrative expenses.

Cons:

- The only liability protection you have will come from buying business insurance.
- You will pay both income and self-employment tax.
- You'll face a higher audit risk than other businesses.

Partnership

A partnership is essentially a combination of sole proprietors. When you start a business with one or more other people, it is automatically considered a partnership whether or not you draft any partnership agreements. Of course, it's in your best interest to speak with an attorney and file some paperwork to precisely define the parameters of the partnership. Otherwise, you may find yourself personally liable for the actions and debts of your partner(s).

In terms of taxes, a partnership is a pass-through entity. This means that all profits are divided among the owners, each of whom pays income and self-employment taxes. Like a sole proprietorship, partnerships offer few tax benefits because of this. They do have the benefit of spreading liability out among two or more people, which can help soften the blow of business debts or litigation.

Pros:

- You'll have relatively low startup costs.
- Little paperwork is required to form the company.
- If there are business debts, you share the liability with your partner(s).

Cons:

- Sharing a business can be challenging, especially if you don't have solid agreements set up in the beginning.

- You pay both income and self-employment taxes on 100 percent of your share of the profits if you actively participate in the business.

- Sharing liability can have negative consequences, since you are responsible for the actions of your partner(s).

Corporation

A corporation is very different from either a partnership or a sole proprietorship. Corporations are their own legal entities. They have their own debts, and taxes are filed independently of the owner. Corporations can be passed down easily from one owner to the next, and in many cases, ownership is divided among multiple investors through the sale of shares.

When you own a share of a company, you hold partial ownership of that company. The dividends that you receive as a shareholder are actually residual profits left over after wages and expenses have been paid. While you're probably most familiar with shares for companies that are publicly traded, privately held companies can sell shares as well, allowing ownership of the business to be spread across multiple shareholders without the personal liability risks inherent in a partnership.

Setting up a corporation is more expensive and time-consuming than other types of businesses, but corporations have more available benefits. There are multiple types of corporations, and each one has its own unique features. Let's dig deeper and see which corporation offers the most tax benefits.

C-Corporation

A C-corporation is the standard or "default" corporate structure for most major businesses. If you own corporate stock, it's almost certainly from a C-corp. The vast majority of major corporations are C-corps because there are no limits to ownership: C-corporations can have as many stockholders as are willing to buy shares in the company.

From a financial perspective, C-corporations have many benefits. The corporation is a separate legal and tax entity, so it has its own tax return and its own deductible expenses. The company's owner is just like any other shareholder, although he probably owns more shares than other investors do.

As the owner of a C-corporation, you pay yourself a salary just as you would pay all your other employees, and those wages are deductible on the corporation's taxes. After all expenses are deducted, the corporation pays taxes based on corporate rates. The remaining money could pass through to shareholders if dividends are. All shareholders pay tax on those dividends, and the corporations are not able to deduct any amount from their tax liability.

C-corporations are your best choice if you ever plan to go public with the company and have its stock traded through the New York Stock Exchange. If you plan to keep the business small, a C-corporation might not be the best bet due to how complicated it can be to establish and run. However, it's worth investigating your options and discussing them with both an attorney and a tax professional to see if a C-corporation would be a good fit for your needs and goals.

Pros:

- You can have as many shareholders as you want.
- The owner does not share liability with the company.
- You have multiple deductible fringe benefits available to claim.
- You would be taxed at a flat rate of just 21% (25% for personal service corporations).

Cons:

- The startup costs for establishing a C-corporation can be high.
- The administrative costs of establishing and running the business are high.
- You are taxed twice if you receive dividends, both on the corporate side and individually.

S-Corporation

An S-corporation is better suited to small, privately held businesses. Unlike a C-corporation, which can have unlimited shareholders, S-corporations are limited to a maximum of 100 shareholders. Additionally, S-corporation shares generally must be held by individuals, whereas C-corporation stock can be held by other corporations and other non-person entities.

What makes an S-corporation attractive is the way distributions are handled. As with a C-corporation, the owner of an S-corporation pays himself a salary. Remaining profits are distributed to shareholders. In an S-corporation, these distributions are not subject to self-employment tax. If you recall the example at the beginning of this chapter, this means that you could cut your self-employment tax significantly. Saving shareholders from double taxation of dividends is another key benefit of an S-corporation over a C-corporation.

Pros:

- You do not share liability with your company.
- Your self-employment taxes are minimized.
- There is no double taxation for shareholders on dividends.

Cons:

- You'll have high startup costs and administrative expenses.
- You can only have 100 shareholders.
- You may not have quite as many deductible expenses and fringe benefits as a C-corporation.

LLC

LLC stands for "Limited Liability Company," and this name makes the primary benefit of this business designation clear. When you own an LLC, you are separate from the company in terms of your financial and legal liability. The unique thing about an LLC is that it can be established for a business of any size, and it can be taxed as any of the above types of entities.

In other words, an LLC can have one employee or a thousand, and its tax strategy can change over time to keep up with the needs of the business. You can establish your sole proprietorship as an LLC today and enjoy limited liability benefits immediately while still being taxed as a sole proprietor. As the business grows, you can change your LLC to be taxed like a corporation, reaping the financial benefits of that strategy.

Thanks to their flexibility, LLCs are very popular choices for startup companies. They do have some weaknesses, so they're not always the perfect option, but they are often the best choice for a new company that has yet to establish itself. To set up an LLC, you will need to consult with an attorney about filling out the appropriate paperwork.

Pros:

- Owners carry limited liability for the company.
- The business's tax structure is flexible.
- An LLC is fairly easy to establish and can be formed with just one employee.

Cons:

- The liability protection is not perfect, especially for single-owner companies.
- An LLC takes more effort to form than a sole proprietorship or partnership, since you will need the help of an attorney.
- There are no inherent tax benefits to an LLC beyond those offered by other types of entities.

Pass Through Business Deduction

The new tax reform law provides for a deduction in the amount of 20% of certain pass-through company income. However, the provision calls for a phase in of a wage and capital limitation for taxpayers with taxable income over a threshold of $157,500 for individuals and $315,000 for joint filers.

In order to apply the wage and capital limitation for taxpayers earning over the threshold, it is first necessary to calculate 20% of the qualified net business income. Each trade or business activity income is calculated separately.

Next, the taxpayer selects the higher of one of two factors. Factor one equals 50% of wages paid and deducted through the company. Factor two consists of the sum of 25% of company wages and 2.5% of qualified unadjusted property. Once the greater of these two factors is determined, the taxpayer uses the lesser of the wage and capital limitation or the percentage of business income factor as their deduction.

Additionally, the same threshold amounts apply to limit a personal service company's ability to participate in the 20% deduction. For personal service pass-through entities whose owners' taxable income exceeds the above-mentioned thresholds, an exclusion of qualified business income and wages are phased in beginning at the threshold limits mentioned and are completely phased in when taxable incomes reach $207,500 for individuals and $415,000 for joint filers.

The method comes as a shock to many voters who assumed tax breaks would not be included in the bill for passive activities like real estate; and one might assume under the wage limitation, that real estate investment companies may not benefit from the provision given they typically have few wages. However, with the ability to use the greater of the 50-percent wage factor or a 25-percent wage plus 2.5-percent capital factor, investors can also benefit from the business income deductions.

Getting the Best Start

As you can see, there are pros and cons to every type of business entity, so there is no simple answer to the question, "Which business entity is best?" You'll need to carefully consider your needs as a business owner and work your way through the maze of options with professionals, taking into account both tax and liability considerations. You may find that the tax benefits of a particular business structure are not worth the start-up and administrative expenses of the business. It may be worthwhile to keep your company as a sole proprietorship or partnership until it grows, then restructure it later once your income and expenses rise. On the other hand, it might be best to form an LLC now and take advantage of its flexibility. All of these options are viable in different situations, and a Certified Tax Coach can help you navigate this maze and make the right decision.

Let's Review the Different Business Entity Pathways:

- Businesses offer a legal tax shelter that allows business owners to grow wealth more efficiently than people who work for others.
- Tax benefits are purposely written into the tax code to reward business owners.
- Choosing the right business entity is a crucial step in developing a smart tax strategy.
- Sole proprietorships and partnerships are the easiest businesses to start, but they offer the fewest tax benefits.
- Corporations offer more tax benefits but are more complex to establish.
- A corporation is its own separate legal entity and pays its own taxes as low as 21%.
- In a C-corporation, you can have unlimited shareholders, and you pay taxes on both your salary and your dividends.
- In an S-corporation, you avoid paying self-employment taxes on distributions, but you lose some of the other benefits of a C-corporation.
- An LLC is a popular choice for startups due to its flexibility.
- Ultimately, you'll want to research your options and discuss them with a tax consultant and an attorney to ensure you're making the best choice.

While you determine the first crucial step in starting your business—choosing a business entity—it is important for you to feel your questions and concerns are being addressed. Everyone has a learning style that works best for them. When asked, a common response from many people will be that they consider themselves visual learners. Thus, the phrase "a picture is worth a thousand words" is worth considering when learning about the different types of business entities. You may want to request that your tax consultant show you a visual of how each choice will work for your business. A flow chart can be very simple, with information on three or four different entities. For highly complex cases, it may be a detailed picture with a myriad of colors, shapes, lines, and arrows that lay out the complicated ownership and income flows amongst different businesses and individuals. If you think this would be helpful for you, let your tax professional know. A Certified Tax Coach will always be willing to do a little extra maze running to make sure you have all the information you need and are confident in your choice of business entity. Remember that good planning is essential to minimizing taxes. When you work your way out of the tax maze by seeking help from the right professionals, you will reap the benefits of the best structure for you. When you minimize your taxes, you maximize your profits!

ABOUT THE AUTHOR

Dale Hammernik, EA, ATA, CTC

Dale Hammernik, President and Owner of Hammernik & Associates, has more than 30 years of experience as a tax and business advisor serving families, individuals, and small businesses in Waukesha and Milwaukee Counties. He is an Enrolled Agent, the highest credential awarded by the IRS, an Accredited Tax Advisor, and a Certified Tax Coach.

According to Dale, "I want my business to set the standard in the tax and accounting industry, providing five-star service and offering expertise that helps others to become more successful. Ninety percent of small businesses fail in the first few years; I do not want any of my clients failing! I believe in educating business owners and providing my clients with actionable and understandable information to help them reach their business and life goals. Success is defining your goals and making them happen."

Dale and his team are continually educating themselves on new developments. "Professional development is extremely important in our industry," he says. "We need to stay ahead of changes, technology, and tax laws because the environment is constantly evolving." Growth oriented businesses should demand the best from their accountants, and we accept that challenge!

A small business owner will wear various hats. It's just impossible to successfully run your business all by yourself, even if you work 24/7. With proper guidance you can take back those hours to find success and enjoy life!

A thought leader in the tax and accounting industry, Dale has appeared on WTMJ-TV's "Live at Daybreak", "Live at Noon," and Fox News broadcasts, and on Milwaukee Public Radio's "Lake Effect." Dale has written blogs on tax issues for BizTimes.com. He has also written a book "Straight Talk about Small Business Success in Wisconsin."

Outside of work, Dale is married to Denise and is a father of three to Nicholas, Marissa, and Jenna. He is contributing to the community and assisting youth in New Berlin. He enjoys coaching youth sports, which allows him to use his business skills to help others achieve success in sports and learn important life lessons.

Dale supports the Muscular Dystrophy Association in various ways by selling shamrocks and donating $1 from each tax return prepared by his firm, along with sponsoring a team in the MDA Walk.

You can connect with Dale via Twitter @HammernikTax, on Facebook at Hammernik & Associate, in person at his West Allis office, or by phone at (414)545-1890.

For more information on Hammernik & Associates, please log on to hammernikassoc.com.

CHAPTER 8

Navigating the Real Estate Tax Maze

BY DANNY FINK, CPA, CTC

Even the savviest investors find the real estate tax maze baffling, often prompting them to choose alternative paths for building wealth. However, no comprehensive investment strategy is complete without the passive income generation potential of real estate. With the right map, you can navigate the real estate tax maze to avoid paying unnecessary taxes and keep more of your income in your wallet.

There are three basic strategies when it comes to making your way through the maze:

- Decrease your taxable income and increase sources of untaxed income.

- Take advantage of applicable tax deductions and tax credits to reduce your tax liability.

- Ensure taxable income qualifies for the lowest possible tax bracket, thereby reducing the rate at which you are taxed.

By investing in real estate and observing these three strategies, you can look forward to finding your way through the real estate tax maze to reach your financial goals.

The Benefits of Braving the Real Estate Tax Maze

The complexity of real estate tax law can be discouraging, but the rewards of navigating this maze are substantial. After all, this type of investing is the world's oldest for a reason. From the Ancient Romans to the first American colonists, people have always pursued the same goal: owning land. Unlike most investment vehicles, real estate generates income twice. First, real estate typically appreciates over time, which means you realize a profit if you decide to sell. Second, permitting others to use the land and buildings generates immediate rental income, which you can then reinvest if you wish. Investment in real estate is unique, as it serves as both a short-term and a long-term investment.

After the U.S. housing bubble burst at the end of 2008, real estate prices dropped dramatically. Many who had invested left the market, never to return. Lower demand means more opportunity for today's real estate investors, as real estate prices remain relatively low—as does competition for the most desirable locations. Better still, the number of people looking for quality rental homes remains high, as members of the millennial generation are waiting much longer than their parents and grandparents did when it comes to purchasing a first home.

Real estate offers a retirement safety net that other types of investments do not. For instance, if you are like most Americans, you are far more likely to make the monthly mortgage payment on your investment property than you are to make regular contributions to your retirement account. It is easier to be disciplined when you get a bill every month. No matter how the real estate market changes, if you keep up with your mortgage payments you will always have the option of keeping your investment properties, which means that you can look forward to reliable rental income after you leave the workforce.

Real Estate Investment, Simplified

In its simplest form, real estate investment involves maximizing profits by choosing a property that is priced on the lower side when compared to similar real estate in the same area. If this isn't possible, focus on reasonably priced real estate in the most desirable neighborhood you can afford. If you are purchasing a home, do the research necessary to ensure the neighborhood has amenities that add value, such as proximity to good schools, easy access to highways, airports, and other methods of transportation, and high-quality recreation facilities. Remember that location is key for real estate investments, and the rate at which your property will appreciate depends on the neighborhood as a whole. Pay attention to demographics, income levels, zoning, and rental trends for the area.

The next step is to rent the property for a reasonable amount—low enough to attract tenants, but high enough to cover the costs of owning and maintaining your property. Ideally, your monthly rental income will actually be high enough to put a bit aside, either to offset your own expenses or to eventually reinvest in additional real estate purchases.

Income you receive from this sort of real estate investment is considered "passive," which means that if you incur a loss, the amount of the loss that you can use to offset other income is limited in most cases. However, there are situations in which your real estate investment income can qualify as "active." Examples include the following:

- If you rent for short periods—seven days or less—the income may qualify as active, since you are essentially running a lodging business.
- If you rent for periods of less than 30 days and you provide each tenant with significant services, the income may qualify as active.
- If you provide "extraordinary" services to your tenants, regardless of how long they stay, you may be actively earning income.
- If the income you receive from renting the property is related to a non-rental activity, it may no longer be passive.
- If the property is used by customers during defined business hours, rental income may be considered active.

- If the property is used in the course of business activities for a business that the property owner also owns, rental income may no longer be passive.

In all of these cases, the change from passive to active income can impact your tax obligations significantly. As a general rule, active income generates more tax benefits than passive income, providing you the opportunity to save on taxes and grow your wealth.

Note that investing in real estate this way is not the same as "flipping" homes for profit. Flipping properties is an entirely different investment method that requires specialized skills. Buyers deliberately purchase a place in need of major renovation. The purchase price is negotiated based on the expected costs of doing the work. People who flip properties have the ability to do the work themselves or have the network needed to get the work done for far less than the estimated renovation cost. Once the property is repaired, flippers sell it right away for a profit. This strategy is typically a short-term investment, while most real estate investments are intended primarily for the long-term.

Those involved in flipping real estate must navigate an entirely different maze of real estate tax regulations, and they miss out on many of the tax benefits available to long-term property investors. Individuals who buy and sell multiple properties in the same year are classified as dealers instead of investors, which impacts how the IRS looks at any income generated. In most cases, those that flip properties find themselves taxed as a business, and profits are considered income instead of capital gains.

Navigate the Real Estate Investment Maze With Smart Financing

The income potential of a single property might not seem significant, but you can look forward to significant profits when you use smart financing for leverage. Increasing real estate investment income starts with expanding the number of properties you own, and financing is the key to your success. Consider this scenario: you are prepared to invest $300,000, so you pay cash to purchase an income property free and clear.

The market will support rental fees of $2,000 per month. Of that amount, you can expect to pay out between $600 and $800 per month for property taxes, insurance, and maintenance. Your profit is between $1,200 and $1,400 per month.

Alternatively, you can invest $100,000 each in three properties, all worth $300,000, by financing the additional $200,000 on each. Your monthly payment for each property is now $1,200 per month, but you are collecting $2,000 in rent from each location. Your profit is $800 for each property, for a total of $2,400 per month—and that is only the short-term investment value. Each of the properties will increase in value over time, so you will eventually realize three times the capital gains.

Most important of all, investment in multiple properties protects your income by spreading out your risk. If something goes wrong in one location—a dramatic neighborhood change that brings property values down or a home that you simply can't keep rented—your other investments will ensure that you continue to have the income you need.

Map to Minimizing Real Estate Tax Obligations

Once you have purchased your properties and the rent payments are rolling in, it is time to focus on navigating your way through the maze of real estate tax regulations. There are a number of ways to save, but you need a map to ensure you are making smart decisions.

Making the Most of Increases in Equity

The first point in your navigation strategy is to carefully consider how you will manage the wealth created by increased property values. For example, if you purchased a home valued at $300,000, and it has increased in value to $350,000, your assets have gone up by $50,000. If you do nothing, you owe nothing in taxes.

Of course, you might want to cash in on some of that increased value—especially if you want to reinvest profits into a new property. One path is to refinance the property, which allows you to cash out your equity without incurring tax obligations.

An alternative option is to sell the property. If you choose to sell an investment property, you can defer any capital gains taxes through the use of a 1031 exchange. A 1031 exchange allows an investor to sell a property, reinvest the proceeds in a new property and defer all capital gains. Using the example from above, an investment property purchased for $300,000 and sold for $350,000 with $100,000 of depreciation taken to date, there would be capital gains of $50,000, plus recapture of the $100,000 of depreciation taken. By using a 1031 exchange, the $50,000 of capital gains and $100,000 of depreciation recapture would be both deferred, saving a total of $35,000 in tax for taxpayers in tax brackets above the 15% bracket.

There are rules and timeframes that must be followed regarding identifying and purchasing the replacement property, so it is advisable to work with a professional familiar with the process if considering a 1031 exchange.

If selling your primary residence, think carefully about when to make the transaction, as a few months can make a difference in whether or not you pay capital gains tax.

You have the option of buying and selling your primary residence once every two years without incurring capital gains taxes. This is particularly relevant if the market has changed significantly, or if you have made any major improvements to the property.

Individuals who own a home are eligible for up to $250,000 in tax-free capital gains, and married couples are eligible for up to $500,000 in tax-free capital gains.

Taking Advantage of Deductions

You are required to pay taxes on your income, but there are a number of caveats in place to ensure you are taxed fairly. For example, you can deduct certain expenses from the amount of your taxable income when the expenses are related to earning that income. A wide variety of deductions specifically apply to real estate, and you can minimize the tax expense by using these regulations to your advantage.

Repairs and maintenance are required to keep buildings habitable, so you can deduct expenses related to regular upkeep of the property. However, it is important to note the difference in how home repairs are treated versus home improvements. Repairing an existing feature of the home isn't intended to increase the property value, while the specific purpose of home improvements is to change basic features of the property for the better. Repairs are usually deductible in the year they are incurred, since they are necessary to earn the income—while home improvements must be capitalized and then depreciated over their useful life.

This point can be important as you make decisions about repair and maintenance projects. For example, all other things equal, repairing a window frame returns it to its original state, while replacing standard windows with specialized energy-saving alternatives is classified as a home improvement. Other examples include replacing existing flooring instead of trading carpet for newly finished hardwoods, and replacing areas of an outdoor deck as needed rather than building a new and improved version.

The most important thing to remember when completing repairs is to keep careful documentation if you plan to deduct the expenses. Make sure receipts are itemized, and get a separate invoice for each project, even if the repairs are completed simultaneously.

Understanding the Nuances of Depreciation

You will face one of the most confusing turns in the maze when it comes time to calculate depreciation. After all, it seems illogical that your property value increases though components of the property are depreciating in value. Nonetheless, the IRS does recognize that parts of your property depreciate every year, some faster than others, and you can deduct this depreciation from your taxable rental income. Making the most of this opportunity requires attention to detail. In general, a commercial building will be depreciated over 39 years while residential rental properties are depreciated over 27.5 years. Keep in mind only the building and improvements are depreciated, not the value of the land.

Generally, your entire building will be depreciated over the same length of time, either 27.5 or 39 years depending on whether it is a residential or commercial property. One way to accelerate your depreciation is through cost segregation. Cost segregation allows you to divide the cost of the building into its various parts, many of which have a much shorter life than 27.5 or 39 years. This allows for larger depreciation amounts earlier in your ownership of the building, saving you money in taxes in the beginning.

The cost segregation study will divide the property into its basic components. For example:

- The home
- Separate but attached structures, such as attached garages
- Detached structures on the property, like sheds, barns, and detached garages
- Land improvements, including finished paths, driveways, and certain types of landscaping
- Specific home features, such as the roof, the cabinets, and the flooring
- Certain appliances, including the furnace and water heater

As you begin to plan repairs and improvements to the property, consider how the rate of depreciation will impact your investment. Research what elements of the home will depreciate more quickly than others. For example, cabinets depreciate more quickly than roofing, so you will recover the outlay of cash for new cabinets sooner than a new roof.

Considering Less Common Tax Credits

Certain properties qualify for less common tax credits, and it is worthwhile to be aware of these when selecting your real estate purchases. One of the most interesting is historical property credits, which support those who purchase and rehabilitate historical structures. These credits may apply to non-residential structures built before 1936, as well as properties that have already been certified as historical sites. Note that credits range from 10 percent to 20 percent, but you may qualify for a larger amount if the property is located in certain qualified disaster areas.

Another category of credits is available for those who are focused on affordable housing projects. There are very specific criteria required to qualify, as the property must meet low-income tenant eligibility and be rent-controlled. These credits only apply to residential real estate.

Using an IRA to Reach the End of the Real Estate Tax Maze

Individual Retirement Accounts (IRAs) are premier tax-advantaged investment products because they are specifically designed to minimize your tax burden when you increase investments earmarked for your retirement. Since you can hold a variety of assets in an IRA, they provide an excellent opportunity to reduce your real estate tax liability while still generating income. There are just a few guidelines to keep you on the right path:

- You must own a self-directed IRA if you wish to purchase real estate with IRA funds.

- The self-directed IRA must be managed by a trustee, who will handle both accounts payable and accounts receivable for your real estate.

- Real estate held in your IRA cannot include any property that you occupy, whether as a primary residence or vacation home. IRA funds must be used to purchase an additional property that you do not currently own.

When you follow this roadmap, your real estate investments will receive the same tax benefits as the rest of your IRA portfolio. Specifically, taxes are deferred until you begin taking distributions from the account. The benefit of this strategy is that most people are in a lower tax bracket when they begin taking distributions from their IRAs, so the total amount of taxes owed is far lower than when the property was initially purchased.

Choosing a New Path: Your Real Estate Business

As you increase your portfolio of properties, you may discover that you have an interest in and a talent for real estate investing. If so, consider the possibility of opening a real estate business, which will improve your investment opportunities and increase the variety of additional tax-reducing strategies available to you. In addition to the deductions and depreciation you might otherwise qualify for when you own an investment property, you will enjoy the many tax advantages of being a small business owner.

If you choose this path, you will be in the business of purchasing and managing rental properties, not selling them, which is an important distinction. As a real estate professional, you could be eligible for the following deductions to lower your tax liability:

- Associated with cleaning a home in preparation for rental and advertising the vacancy.

- Home office expenses if you have a dedicated office space for your business in your residence.

- Wages and benefits you pay to employees who work for your business.

- Professional services you hire to assist with business needs. These may include lawyers, accountants, financial advisors, etc.

- Travel expenses related to managing the rental properties. Examples include mileage and overnight accommodations when necessary.

- Meal and entertainment expenses incurred as a cost of doing business. For example, if you take a prospective tenant to lunch, you may be able to deduct the bill as a business expense.

- Mortgage interest charged for repair and improvement expenses, as well as the mortgage interest charged when you purchase related equipment.

- The cost of property insurance and other insurance associated with your real estate business.

There are several other simple techniques to maximize the expenses you can deduct, which is well worth the effort. Through application of appropriate tax deductions, you reduce your taxable income. This brings down the amount you owe to the IRS, so more of your money stays in your pocket.

One of the lesser-known yet most valuable tax deductions is hiring family members to staff your business. By hiring employees and offering benefits, you qualify for deductions that don't apply to you as an individual investor, while reducing the amount of work you have to complete on your own. If you are paying your children as business employees, the first $12,000 does not incur taxes—a huge benefit for those new to the working world.

New for 2018

The new tax reform law provides for a deduction in the amount of 20% of certain pass-through company income. However, the provision calls for a phase in of a wage and capital limitation for taxpayers with taxable income over a threshold of $157,500 for individuals and $315,000 for joint filers.

In order to apply the wage and capital limitation for taxpayers earning over the threshold, it is first necessary to calculate 20% of the qualified net business income. Each trade or business activity income is calculated separately.

Next, the taxpayer selects the higher of one of two factors. Factor one equals 50% of wages paid and deducted through the company. Factor two consists of the sum of 25% of company wages and 2.5% of qualified unadjusted property. Once the greater of these two factors is determined, the taxpayer uses the lesser of the wage and capital limitation or the percentage of business income factor as their deduction.

The method comes as a shock to many voters who assumed tax breaks would not be included in the bill for passive activities like real estate; and one might assume under the wage limitation, that real estate investment companies may not benefit from the provision given they typically have few wages. However, with the ability to use the greater of the 50% wage factor or a 25% wage plus 2.5% capital factor, investors can also benefit from the business income deductions.

Once your investment in real estate transitions from a passive source of income to an active business, your tax status changes. You will have the opportunity to claim business losses to offset gains from other sources of income. There are quite a few requirements that you must meet to qualify for this type of deduction, but when you do, it is possible to dramatically reduce your taxable income.

Investing in real estate is critical to growing your wealth, and when you choose to turn your investment strategy into a business, the tax advantages increase. Avoid pitfalls when navigating the real estate tax maze by relying on expert guides such as a Certified Tax Coach and a specialized financial advisor. These professionals can assist you in making the most of your investment portfolio to achieve your financial goals.

ABOUT THE AUTHOR

Danny Fink, CPA, CTC

My name is Danny Fink, I am the owner and founder of Premier Tax Consulting LLC. I'm also a CPA and Certified Tax Coach. I am one of approximately 400 tax professionals in the country to earn this elite designation.

I started Premier Tax Consulting to offer a different kind of service. We don't just record the history you give us when we file taxes for you. We go beyond that by offering you proactive advice and strategies to help you earn more and keep more.

Premier Tax Consulting was the 2014 Best of Morgantown Award Winner for Tax Planning Services, and I am a Dave Ramsey Endorsed Local Provider for Tax Services.

I am a long-time endurance athlete and was a member of the United States Summer Biathlon National Team for 10 years. I represented the United States at eight World Championships, winning two medals in international competition as a member of Team USA.

I live in Morgantown, WV with my wife Leah and our two sons, Alex and Ben.

Danny Fink, CPA, CTC

Premier Tax Consulting, LLC

69 Clay Street, Suite 101

Morgantown, WV 26501

danny@premiertaxwv.com

www.premiertaxwv.com

(888)505-6592

CHAPTER 9

The Twists and Turns of Cost Segregation

BY GYANESH MATHUR, CPA, CTC

Maneuvering the tax maze is complicated at best, and it is common to discover that there are tax minimization tactics you have completely omitted from your long-term strategy. Cost segregation is a prime example. It is one of the more complex elements of tax regulation, and it can be difficult to apply properly without the assistance of an accountant and a Certified Tax Coach. However, putting the time and effort into cost segregation is well worth your while, as you can realize significant tax benefits. Remember, when you are making your way through the tax maze, using every available technique can help you reach your destination with your wealth intact.

The Basics of Cost Segregation

The first step to making cost segregation a part of your tax minimization strategy is clearly understanding what it is—and what it isn't. You are probably familiar with the concept of depreciation, which allows you to measure the useful life of an asset, then deduct the expense of its declining value over time. When it comes to real estate, the useful life can be long. For example, non-residential buildings are typically depreciated over 39 years. However, that doesn't necessarily mean that all components of the property should be held to the 39-year depreciation period.

Cost segregation is intended for commercial real estate, which is any property that you own with the intention of generating a profit. While residential real estate that you purchase and subsequently rent to others is not commercial real estate, its status as an income-producing residential property qualifies it for shorter depreciation periods than other commercial property. Current tax regulations set the standard depreciation period for residential real assets at 27.5 years.

Owners of commercial buildings have certain responsibilities, including basic management and upkeep. In addition, they handle the financial aspects of owning real estate, such as paying taxes, purchasing and maintaining insurance, and arranging for appropriate accounting services. The total commercial real estate package includes land, buildings, and any improvements that are purchased or constructed on the property. Some examples include warehouses, manufacturing facilities, hotels, offices, and shopping centers. These are often referred to as "real property."

Cost segregation is the process of examining all aspects of a real asset to tease out elements that qualify as personal property assets rather than real property assets for the purpose of tax reporting. Personal property and land improvements are depreciated much more quickly, between five and fifteen years, which means a much bigger impact on your deductible expenses. Of course, the higher your deductions, the less taxable income you have, so you can look forward to lower overall tax liability.

Though the savings realized through cost segregation can be significant, many property owners don't take advantage of this method, primarily because the specifics of when and how to use it are not clearly spelled out. Generally speaking, cost segregation practices have developed over time as a result of IRS rulings, rather than being available as a list of requirements in a section of the tax code.

Myths and Facts: The IRS View of Cost Segregation

Because detailed procedures for cost segregation aren't clearly outlined in IRS regulations, there is a misperception among business owners that choosing cost segregation is considered an "aggressive" stance by the IRS. Nothing could be further from the truth. In decision after decision, the IRS has made it clear that cost segregation is the correct method of calculating depreciation.

The IRS does, however, care deeply about the methodology used to classify personal and real property. The agency has published a comprehensive guide to approved cost segregation study practices, which can be found on the IRS website under IRS Cost Segregation Audit Techniques Guide. When you hire a qualified Cost Segregation Professional who conducts a cost segregation study using standard methods, you don't have to worry about running afoul of the IRS.

The Purpose of Cost Segregation Studies

Generally, personal property consists of the non-structural elements of a building, along with indirect construction costs and exterior land improvements. For example, features that are attached to your building may qualify as personal property if they do not contribute to the operation or maintenance of the building. The process of separating personal and real property is referred to as a cost segregation study.

The nuances of separating personal and real property are often best left to the professionals, as the process includes an in-depth examination of financial and engineering records. Your Certified Tax Coach can provide more details on securing the most qualified specialist for the job. Through cost segregation studies, you often learn that unexpected features of your property fall under the personal category, which gives you an opportunity to accelerate depreciation and enjoy tax savings.

Consider this example:

You purchase a warehouse for your business in the amount of $2 million, with 15 percent of the value coming from the land. That means you can depreciate $1.7 million over 39 years. However, through a cost segregation study, you determine that $225,000 of your total purchase price qualifies as land improvements, which can be depreciated over fifteen years. An additional $200,000 of your purchase price is considered property that can be depreciated over five years. In total, rather than deducting depreciation expense for $1.7 million over 39 years, only $1.275 is drawn out that long. A large portion, $425,000 or 25%, can be depreciated more quickly, minimizing your tax expense in the early years of owning the building.

The most common cost segregation opportunities include the following:

- **Purchase of an existing property** – Primarily when the building is valued at $500,000 or more, excluding land.

- **New construction** – Primarily when the building is valued at $500,000 or more, excluding land.

- **Expansion or renovations** – Primarily when the cost of expansion or renovations is $500,000 or more.

- **Leasehold improvements** – When commercial real estate owners lease their property to tenants, the tenants often require certain improvements and renovations to ensure the space meets the needs of their businesses. Generally, tenants are responsible for making the necessary changes to the property, even though they do not own the building. Unless otherwise negotiated in the lease, tenants have use of any improvements they make for the duration of their occupancy. However, once they vacate the property, ownership of the improvements transfers to the property owner. As long as the improvements are made at least three years after the building is placed into service and the owner and tenant are not related, owners may be able to realize tax savings on improvements made by the tenant through cost segregation.

- **Real property stepped up through estate** – Though a property might be fully depreciated during the original owner's lifetime, the process of transferring ownership through an estate can restart the depreciation clock. The tax basis of the real estate is typically stepped up or increased to fair market value, and the new owner begins the process of depreciation once again.

- **Look-backs on existing property placed in service after 1986** – Though prior tax years might be closed, IRS regulations permit you to go back and claim missed depreciation as far as 1987. You can do this without amending your tax returns.

You can conduct a cost segregation study at any point, though you are likely to realize the greatest benefits when you start classifying assets as soon as the building is purchased or built. In certain cases, your Cost Segregation Professional might recommend a pre-construction evaluation, which takes place before the building's infrastructure is put in place.

Eligibility for Tax Benefits

There are a few factors to consider before committing to a cost segregation study. Though separating assets into the appropriate categories usually leads to tax savings, the benefits don't always outweigh the costs, and not everyone is guaranteed a lower tax bill. These are the five questions to ask before moving forward:

- **How is the business structured?** The legal entity you have selected for your business can impact whether you see a change in your taxes as a result of your cost segregation study, and you might not have sufficient tax basis to benefit from accelerated depreciation deductions. For example, if your business is an S-Corporation with limited shareholders, you may be restricted in the amount of tax losses you can report. C-Corporations with net operating losses will also limit tax benefits of accelerated depreciation, making it unnecessary to conduct a cost segregation study.

- **What is your strategy for the property?** If you expect to sell the building soon, a cost segregation study is unlikely to offer any useful benefits. You can increase your depreciation deductions until you sell, but then you will be responsible for recapture of those tax benefits shortly thereafter.

- **What is the nature of your business?** Depending on the type of business you operate, passive activity loss (PAL) rules may limit your ability to apply the increased deductions right away. Carefully examine the impact of PAL rules on your tax calculations before investing in a cost segregation study.

- **Are you subject to the alternative minimum tax?** If you are, you may not be able to use the increased deductions right away, in which case a cost segregation study is an unnecessary expense.
- **What is the value of the building?** Most Cost Segregation Professionals recommend investing in a cost segregation study when the value of commercial real estate is $1 million or more, excluding the value of the land. However, there can be benefits for those who spend at least $500,000 on buildings, building expansions, and renovations.

Determining whether you can benefit from accelerated depreciation is an important first step in the cost segregation study process.

Choosing a Skilled Cost Segregation Professional

Once you and your Certified Tax Coach have agreed that you can benefit from a cost segregation study, enlist assistance from a qualified Cost Segregation Professional. These individuals have experience and expertise in a range of fields, making them uniquely capable of conducting a thorough, accurate study. Some of the most critical qualifications include the following:

- Knowledge and experience in construction and engineering is needed to evaluate building features and classify them in the correct categories for depreciation purposes.
- Deep understanding of tax regulations, as well as up-to-date knowledge of changes in the law, ensures that all determinations are made in accordance with IRS rules.
- Knowledge of relevant court cases supports your Cost Segregation Professional's ability to make an accurate assessment of your property. As case law has demonstrated repeatedly, the exact

same asset can be classified differently based on the circumstances surrounding its purchase.

- Compliance with the IRS Audit Techniques Guide ensures you won't run any risk of taking deductions you are not entitled to. Your Cost Segregation Professional should be well-versed in the criteria contained in the guide and capable of applying the principles to real-world situations.

Although not required, it is particularly helpful if the individual conducting your cost segregation study is familiar with other strategies for minimizing tax liability. Many business owners have realized additional savings when, in the course of their cost segregation study, the Cost Segregation Professional identified other areas that should be examined for potential tax savings. Examples include Abandonment Studies and Fixed Asset Studies.

Conducting a Cost Segregation Study

A complete cost segregation study takes time, during which you can expect your specialist to complete the following activities:

- A visual inspection of the property takes place, so the Cost Segregation Professional can note any special features of the building or unique aspects of the construction. Be prepared to discuss these in detail—they are important to the overall analysis.

- The Cost Segregation Professional will examine the purpose and function of any features that could potentially be considered non-structural building components or tangible personal property for tax depreciation purposes.

- All of the documentation you have gathered, including appraisal reports, as-built drawings, and blueprints will be collected and reviewed by the Cost Segregation Professional. The specialist will analyze the data and use the information when categorizing assets.

- Typically, these professionals photograph any components of the building that could qualify as non-structural building components or tangible personal property to create a visual record of those features.

- Once all of the information and documentation has been thoroughly examined, the Cost Segregation Professional will complete a list of items that meet the criteria for non-structural building components or tangible personal property as it is related to tax regulations.

- The specialist will also consider whether certain owner-incurred costs qualify as non-structural building components or tangible personal property.

At this point in the process, the data-gathering phase is complete. The next step is to document findings and determine how depreciation regulations should be applied. Your Cost Segregation Professional will manage the following tasks:

- Completion of a schedule that lists each qualifying item, the direct costs for the items, and the allocable fees and overhead items.

- The schedule will specify the appropriate cost recovery periods, and the Cost Segregation Specialist will use resources from the IRC, existing regulations, court opinions, and IRS rulings to clarify each item's cost recovery life.

- Because the findings of a cost segregation study impact the work of the company's Certified Financial Manager (CFM), Certified Tax Coach, and Certified Public Accountant (CPA), most Cost Segregation Professionals partner with them to coordinate the reconciliation of all identified costs to the accounting ledgers.

- The Cost Segregation Professional usually works with other members of the finance team to complete any necessary IRS paperwork such as the IRS Form 3115, Application for Change in Accounting Method, and related schedules. In addition, these specialists complete a written report that details the conclusions from the investigation and analysis in a format that complies with IRS documentation requirements.

Finally, at the end of the process you can expect the most important document of all—a calculation of the tax savings you will realize as a result of your investment in a cost segregation study.

Cost Segregation Results

Industry experts have compiled and analyzed data that show the average rates of reallocation for a variety of property types. While the results of cost segregation studies vary widely, these figures offer a general overview of how cost segregation could impact your tax liability:

Apartments	20 – 35%
Car Dealerships	25 – 50%
Golf Courses	20 – 40%
Grocery Stores	20 – 30%
Hotels and Motels	20 – 30%
Manufacturing and Processing (Heavy)	30 – 60%
Manufacturing (Light)	20 – 40%
MOB'S/MAB'S	20 – 40%
Offices	20 – 40%
Research and Development	30 – 60%
Restaurants	20 – 40%
Retail	20 – 30%
Senior and Assisted Living	15 – 25%
Strip Malls and Regional Malls	5 – 30%
Tenant Improvements	5 – 50%
Theaters	20 – 30%
Warehouses	5 – 10%

Depending on the value of your property and where it falls in these ranges, your first-year savings can easily reach $1 million or more.

Though cost segregation is a complex field, don't let potential tax savings slip by. Your Certified Tax Coach and your Cost Segregation Professional can ensure you maximize your depreciation expense to minimize your tax liability. Bear in mind that it is never too late to take advantage of these potential savings. IRS regulations allow you up to 30 years of look-back to claim any depreciation you missed.

ABOUT THE AUTHOR

Gyanesh Mathur, CPA, CTC

Gyanesh Mathur, CPA, CTC, CTRS, CHBC, FCA specializes in advanced tax planning strategies for businesses. He is the founder of Aeon Capital Consultants which performs Engineered Cost Segregation studies. In this book, he covers this valuable tax planning tool.

In many years of working with this lucrative tax strategy, his engineering team has performed cost segregation studies for hotels, office buildings, manufacturing plants, restaurants, retail centers, warehouses, medical office buildings and many others. The extensive experience of the engineering team and knowledge of current legislation, regulations, revenue rulings, and court cases provides clients with a thorough and supportable analysis. The methodologies and procedures employed rely on fully documented engineering and appraisal techniques.

Gyanesh Mathur specializes in health care. His team is acutely aware of the rapidly changing landscape in the health care field and its impact on your business. The team of professionals are health care certified and have the knowledge and experience to factor in all the variables to help grow your practice and profits from the day you open your doors to the day you retire.

Gyanesh can be contacted at:

Aeon Capital Consultants
3900 Newpark Mall Road
Third Floor
Newark, CA 94560
t: 510-257-4000 f: 408-228-1931
www.aeoncap.com

CHAPTER 10

The Map to Hidden Business Deductions

BY DIANA V. CASTRO, EA, CTC

Getting through the tax maze with minimal tax liability is a challenge, and you often have to take unexpected twists and turns to meet your goal. While deducting business expenses may seem straightforward on the surface, there are a number of nuances that—when applied appropriately—can dramatically change your final bill.

Taking advantage of all the business deductions you are entitled to requires assistance from an expert Certified Tax Coach. Though accountants and tax advisors provide a valuable service, they specialize in routine tax matters. Often, they work through a high volume of tax returns, and they use a proven method to complete forms accurately and efficiently. Unfortunately, too much routine can result in missing important opportunities for tax savings not only in a current tax year, but for many years to come.

Mapping out hidden business deductions is an important part of your comprehensive tax strategy. We'll review some of the most common missed opportunities, but first, you must be sure to heed the advice below.

Avoiding Traps in the Tax Maze

Tax regulations are extremely complex, and you don't want to run afoul of the law. While there are loopholes that may allow you to enjoy extra tax savings, make sure you consult an expert to avoid any legal traps. The loopholes exist to encourage very specific business-related behaviors, such as increasing the number of small businesses through tax incentives. You may not qualify for every deduction and exemption, and it is unwise to take deductions you are not entitled to. Those who do can find themselves in audit territory, resulting in not only a whole lot of stress, but also in paying quite a bit in interest, penalties, and fees.

Taking a Closer Look at Your Expenses

You are already deducting many of your business expenses, which means that you don't have to pay taxes on those funds. Examples of common deductions include utilities, equipment, and the cost of inventory. However, you are likely spending quite a bit more on other items and activities that you aren't deducting, because the path to deduction is less obvious. Understanding how additional expenses can qualify as deductions is the secret to bringing your tax liability down. The first step is to carefully record your spending, so you know exactly where every penny is going. Next, consider whether any of your expenses fall into the categories that follow.

Home Office

As every small business owner knows, there is no such thing as "off-the-clock" when you are an entrepreneur. Though you might usually work from an office on the premises of your business, chances are that you complete vital business-related activities from home as well. Creating a formal space to conduct business-related activities in your home could qualify you for deductions related to a home office. This effectively reduces the cost of your mortgage, rent, and utilities in your personal budget.

Start-Up and Organizational Expenses

When you start a business, the costs associated with building something brand-new are often quite high. You have to purchase all of the initial equipment and inventory, secure and prepare the business location, and grab the attention of prospective customers. In fact, these start-up and organizational expenses are one of the primary reasons that many people are unable to get their business ideas off the ground. The initial financial burden is simply too high.

The government wants to encourage entrepreneurs to open and expand their small businesses, so a special deduction was created. You can deduct up to $10,000 of your start-up and organizational costs in the first year that you are in operation. In addition to equipment, inventory, and similar expenses, you can include fees associated with establishing a legal partnership or incorporating. Most interesting of all, within this $10,000 limit, you can deduct the costs associated with the research you did before taking the plunge. For example, if you spent hundreds on developing a new process that simplifies how an item is manufactured, you can claim this amount as a deduction.

Purchases for Your Start-Up

In addition to deducting up to $10,000 in start-up and organizational expenses, there is another opportunity for new business owners to save on their taxes. If you purchase equipment for the business, i.e. computers, copy machines, and other miscellaneous necessary items, you can choose to take the full depreciation in your first year of business. This option only applies to items that you purchased new for the business with your own funds, and there is a cap on the total amount you can deduct. The alternative is to depreciate the items over time, as you will with any future purchases you make after your first year in business.

Remember that the IRS has a very specific definition as far as the official start of a business. In essence, you start a business when you have all of the tools and equipment necessary to perform the intended function of the business and you are actively available to perform that function, whether or not you have any clients or you have made a sale. For instance, if you are a lawyer, your business begins when you are officially available for hire, even if no one hires you right away. If you are a writer, your business begins when you start writing, not when you have sold a manuscript.

Vehicles

The deduction you can take for a vehicle purchase depends on the type of vehicle you buy for your business, so it is important to consider the needs of your business and the tax advantages of different types of vehicles before you make a decision. Adding to the complexity is choosing whether to buy or lease. Standard cars and light trucks qualify for a smaller deduction than heavy vehicles like pick-up trucks and vans. SUVs fall in somewhere in the middle. Deductions on new vehicle purchases in the first year can vary substantially between vehicles that are under and over a cut-off weight of 6,000 pounds.

Marketing

Spreading the word about your new business can be a lot of fun, particularly when you take advantage of new digital marketing options. Creating social media ads, shooting quick videos, printing business cards, and producing brochures are critical steps to attracting customers. Unfortunately, they can get quite expensive. Many small business owners don't realize that many of these expenses can be deducted, and not just the obvious hard costs of printing. If you hire someone to handle your graphic design or you incur expenses when purchasing equipment to shoot video content for your blog, you may be able to deduct those items as well.

Training and Development

Establishing and growing your business requires certain knowledge and skills, many of which you already have. However, there is always new information available, as well as opportunities to enhance your existing abilities. Don't pass up a chance to take a class, attend a seminar, or participate in a convention because of the cost. Training and development is often a deductible expense. This also applies to the purchase of books related to your field, subscriptions to trade magazines, and the dues you pay to professional organizations.

Wellness Activities

Many small businesses offer employees an opportunity to use on-site fitness equipment. This is a nice perk, particularly when the budget won't allow for more costly benefits. If you have incorporated your business and all of your employees are eligible to use this equipment, the cost of maintenance may be a deductible business expense.

Keep in mind that business tax laws change frequently, and deductions that were available to you in the past may no longer apply. On the other hand, new deductions can also be added at any time. You can ensure you are taking advantage of all available opportunities to save on your taxes by consulting your Certified Tax Coach.

Include Your Family in the Journey

Chances are, you are already providing substantial financial support to at least one family member. In many cases, the number is much higher. Today's business owners often find themselves in the "sandwich generation," caring for aging parents as well as children. Hiring family members to work for you can result in substantial deductions, making it much easier to get through the tax maze.

Retirement Savings

If your spouse doesn't have access to an employer-sponsored retirement savings plan, then it is likely that you are allocating funds into a traditional or Roth IRA. While these retirement programs have tax advantages, you can increase your tax savings by employing your spouse. In addition to the tax benefits from your spouse's contributions to the plan, your business can also save money in taxes by making contributions.

Social Security and Medicare Taxes

If you are a sole proprietor or you run a partnership in which you and your spouse are the only partners, you may be able to realize considerable savings on Social Security and Medicare taxes by hiring your children. As long as they are under the age of 18, they may not be required to pay Social Security and Medicare, which means your business benefits along with them.

Unemployment Taxes

Hiring your children who are under the age of 21 can mean significant savings in unemployment taxes as well. While your business would be responsible for unemployment taxes for any other employee, there is a special provision that takes effect when your children work for you. This same provision applies to hiring spouses; you are not required to pay unemployment taxes for them either, as long as you do not have any other non-family partners with an ownership interest in the business.

Keep in mind that the tax benefits of hiring family members are not intended to be taken lightly. To qualify for the various exemptions, each family member on the payroll must be employed in a real job, doing actual work that adds value to the business. The salary and wages paid to family members working for you must be appropriate for the position. For example, you cannot pay your daughter $50,000/year to complete basic clerical work if your highest paid skilled technician receives an annual salary of that amount or less.

Recordkeeping is critical if you are ever asked for proof that your family members performed services for the business. Keep track of job descriptions, responsibilities, and examples of completed projects— along with payroll records—just to be sure you can show that you are complying with IRS regulations.

Employee Incentives and Awards

Creating and maintaining a strong company culture is important to keeping your employees engaged in their work, and studies have shown over and over again that engaged employees are more productive. Many small business owners use personal funds to recognize and reward staff members for a job well done. However, using your personal funds for these incentives isn't necessary. Many types of employee recognition and reward can qualify as deductible business expenses.

Service Anniversaries

Celebrate your staff members' years of service with special recognition and perhaps a little gift. Every five years, you can deduct the cost of a length of service award for an employee, as long as it is not cash, and it is valued at $400 or less. A weekend getaway, a meal at a local restaurant, or a lovely wristwatch could easily meet these criteria.

Meals and Snacks

The most popular way to reward employees is still through their taste buds, and ordering lunch on particularly stressful days or celebrating a job well done with pizza is a great way to show appreciation. As long as these expenses are reasonable, you are usually able to deduct them.

Special Occasions

A birthday isn't a birthday without a card signed by all of your co-workers, and around the holidays, many employers like to spread a bit of cheer. Small, non-cash gifts valued at less than $25 may be tax deductible as business expenses. Along the same lines, you can recognize staff members' important life events, such as a new baby or a death in the family, with flowers. Again, if the value is under $25, you are often able to deduct this as a business expense.

Your employees are important partners as you make your way through the tax maze. Take a moment to recognize their contributions to your success, then take advantage of the tax benefits related to employee incentives and rewards.

More Hidden Business Deductions

Some of the most valuable tax deductions are hidden within activities you do every day. Rethinking your approach can reduce your tax liability significantly. The list below shows just a few of the ways smart taxpayers benefit from hidden business deductions.

Business Meals

Eating out is part of today's busy lifestyles, and stopping for a cup of coffee is an everyday habit for many people. When you have meals with potential clients and you discuss business at some point before, during, or after it, 50% of the expense is deductible. You can even invite a colleague to join you for a meal or coffee and take advantage of the deduction as long as you follow that same guideline. While this might not seem like much day-to-day, your savings can really add up over the course of a year.

Hobbies

Having fun in the course of doing business is often one of the main reasons people decide to explore self-employment. After all, you can choose your own hours, and you determine where and how the work is done. In many cases, the business is a reflection of personal interests, combining favorite pastimes with opportunities to increase income. You might be surprised to discover that many hobbies—when paired with business activities—involve deductible expenses. If you can combine the two, you may be able to save on your taxes.

The primary difference between a business and a hobby, is the pursuit of a profit. Most hobbies are undertaken because the taxpayer finds the activities enjoyable, but even if profit is not achieved, they will still participate in the hobby. By actively pursuing a profit and running the activity as a legitimate business, you can turn your hobby into a profit center.

Another popular way to turn expensive hobbies into opportunities for tax savings is to write a business plan for your hobby. For example, if you produce a craft, you may be able to sell some of your work through craft fairs or online craft sites. As long as you have a viable business plan and you show your financial projections, your hobby could qualify as a business, meaning related expenses turn into tax deductions. And if you are successful in turning a profit, you have the extra benefit of additional income.

Travel

The traveling you do for your business can be deducted as an expense, and there are no rules that prohibit you from bringing family along, although the cost of their travel may not qualify for tax deductions. By combining business-related activities with your family vacation, you can trim some of the expenses associated with both. Take care to keep detailed records of the trip's business purpose, and ensure that the business expenses you submit are reasonable.

Getting creative when it comes to business expenses is critical to getting all of the deductions you are entitled to, and there is no one-size-fits-all approach. Work with your Certified Tax Coach to create a customized plan that ensures you are making the most of all available opportunities to save on your taxes. Enjoy your job, your life, and your appropriate expense deductions!

ABOUT THE AUTHOR

Diana V. Castro, CTC

Diana Castro is the founder and President of Legacy Tax Services, a tax preparation and tax planning firm. She is also the Principal Broker/Owner of Legacy Lending Services, Inc., an independent mortgage firm located in Ventura, CA.

Ms. Castro is a published author and has been featured in several books. She specializes in mortgage and tax planning for individuals, real estate professionals, investors, and small to medium sized businesses. For over 20 years, Diana has provided tax, mortgage, and business consulting services worldwide to individuals, small businesses, and large corporations. She has led seminars and educational workshops on various topics with titles including: Improving Organization Performance, Behavior-Based Strategies, The Basics to Home Buying, Women and Investing, Wealth Management, Quadrant Living, Short Sales, Buying REO properties, Credit Scoring and Improvement, and Local and Federal Grant Programs for Homebuyers.

Ms. Castro is a graduate of University of California, Santa Barbara. She is a native Californian and is fluent in Spanish and French. Ms. Castro loves being a mother to her two grown daughters. She also has several rescue cats and dogs. She enjoys international traveling, reading, researching, beach time, walking, running, real estate investing, and home remodeling projects.

Ms. Castro can be reached at: 805-650-1052 x224, or Diana@legacy-taxes.com

CHAPTER 11

Succession Planning: Start with the Finish in Mind

BY DAVID AUER, MS, PFS

When you start your business, your focus is getting it off the ground. Once production is moving along at a steady clip, your focus is on expansion. With so much time and energy spent on growing the business, many entrepreneurs forget to plan their exit strategy. Even if you have taken all of the right turns through the tax maze, failure to prepare for passing your company on can lead to significant tax expense for you, your shareholders, and your family. The last thing you want is to hand over a large portion of your wealth to tax collectors when you leave the organization.

Starting your succession planning when you open your business is the best way to ensure that the value you build through years of hard work remains intact. By utilizing the strategies set forth in this chapter, you'll get on the right path to turning a comfortable profit when you sell your business or find out what steps you should take to leave it to your beneficiaries while keeping taxes at a bare minimum. Include your exit plans as part of your comprehensive tax savings strategy, so that you are always prepared for major life events—even if they are completely unexpected.

Exit Strategy Options

Managing your company for the purpose of building value for share-holders requires very different methods than creating a profitable business to fund your current lifestyle. Understanding your exit strategy options and choosing a long-term goal will ensure that you stay on the right path throughout your time with the organization.

These are the most common ways business owners manage—and leave—their companies, along with the impact each option has on building long-term wealth through tax savings.

Building a Lifestyle Business

If the primary reason you want to own a business is to fund your personal expenses, you are probably more concerned with current profitability than long-term growth. Individuals with this sort of company typically structure the organization in a manner that allows them to transfer profits to themselves for personal use. Of course, this sort of structure isn't appropriate if your company has other shareholders. Without an agreement to the contrary, shareholders typically expect to enjoy a portion of the profits as well.

Pulling all of the profits out of your company to fund your day-to-day living expenses means that you are not reinvesting in the business. Eventually, this strategy leads to an organization with very little value, so when you are ready to move on, the only option is to close your doors for good. Living off of your company's income doesn't offer much in the way of tax savings. You won't be able to take advantage of the many tax deductions intended to help you grow and expand the business, and you will be responsible for income taxes on the amount you receive in salary and bonuses. If you choose to move forward with a lifestyle business, be sure to examine opportunities for tax savings in other areas of your finances.

Sharing Your Success with Family Members

Building a strong, profitable business can leave a lasting legacy, particularly if you choose to pass the company on to a family member when you retire or pass away. This method of exiting the business can result in significant financial benefits for you and your beneficiaries. However, there are several points to consider before transferring ownership of your company to a member of your family.

- Have any family members expressed an interest in owning your business?

- If so, does the individual possess the knowledge and skills to be successful?

- Will the selection of one family member to the exclusion of other loved ones be disruptive to family unity?

- Are there non-family members who reasonably expect to be included in your future business plans? Examples include business partners and key employees who have devoted their careers to your company's success.

Examine your priorities before making your final decision, as your goals might not be compatible. If your primary concern is to leave the business in good hands so it will continue to be profitable for many years, choosing an interested but inexperienced family member as the new owner is unlikely to be successful.

Once you have determined that passing your business on to a member of your family is the best decision, the next step is to decide how the transaction will occur. There are three main methods of transferring ownership to a family member. First, you can sell your business to a member of your family in the same way you would sell to any other buyer. Next, you can give the business to one or more family members as a gift. Finally, you can retain ownership throughout your lifetime, passing ownership to your beneficiaries after your death.

Your tax liability changes depending on which method you choose, so it is important to examine the pros and cons of each option carefully.

For instance, gifting your business or including it in your estate may result in the expense of both gift and estate taxes. However, you may not have to pay capital gains taxes in these situations.

Your Certified Tax Coach has the expertise necessary to determine how you can minimize tax liability for everyone involved. One of the most effective options for keeping taxes low when transferring business ownership to family members is the creation of a Family Limited Partnership (FLP). To do this, your company must be an LLC, a Limited Partnership, or an S Corporation. You can give shares in the company to family members as a gift, at which point they take on the liability for any related taxes. If you choose to gift shares over time, you may have an opportunity to avoid gift taxes by staying under the annual gifting threshold each year.

Closing the Sale

Sometimes, giving or selling your business to a family member simply doesn't make sense. Either you don't have relatives with an interest in owning the company, or there aren't any family members with the skills necessary for successful business operation. In this situation, most business owners elect to sell the company when they are ready to retire.

From a practical perspective, selling your business can be the cleanest, simplest exit strategy. The buyer has an opportunity to become a business owner without taking the risks that come with entrepreneurship, and you can pocket your profits and walk away, completely free of any future business-related responsibilities. In fact, starting businesses with the intention of growing them for future sale is a viable method of making a living for many entrepreneurs who want to explore a variety of ideas and industries over the course of their careers.

There are two primary ways to transfer ownership of your business. First, you can sell the company outright, as you would sell any other product or service. Once the papers are signed and money changes hands, you are free to move on. The second method of transferring ownership of your business is through acquisition by another organization.

The other organization benefits from acquiring companies versus building expansions from the ground up, because established companies start bringing in money right away.

The latter transaction tends to be more complex, as well as far more disruptive to current employees and clients. Generally, the company making the acquisition has policies and procedures in place already, along with branding and marketing requirements. Your company will be expected to conform, and in just a few short months, it could look very different from the business that you built.

Choosing whether you will sell your business outright or as part of an acquisition may depend on who shows interest in purchasing the company and at what price. If your priority is to get the best possible return on the investment you have put into your business over many years, then you may not be concerned with other factors. In this case, an acquisition could be the most profitable way to exit the business, as companies in a position to acquire others tend to have enough money to make a strong offer.

If you are as concerned with leaving your company in good hands as you are with getting the best possible sales price, you may wish to consider the following:

- What are the prospective buyers' plans for your customers and employees? For some business owners, ensuring current staff and clients are well cared for is first and foremost on the priority list.

- Is the prospective buyer passionate about your business? Does he or she have the qualifications to operate it successfully? If so, you can trust that your legacy will be preserved. As an added benefit, buyers who have a personal interest in your business are likely to make a higher offer.

- How will the buyer finance the purchase? In many cases, transfers of ownership are seller-financed, and they take place over a period of time. If this isn't what you had in mind, making sure the buyer can pay up-front is an important factor to consider.

One caveat when it comes to making the final sale: it isn't wise to drastically change your business to meet the requirements of a prospective buyer. Though correcting certain fundamental issues is perfectly sensible, customizing your operation to impress a single potential purchaser can backfire if the deal falls through. Changes you made at the request of the previous buyer may not be attractive to alternative buyers.

Selling to Shareholders

The number of publicly traded companies is minuscule when compared to the millions of small, privately owned businesses in the United States. Occasionally, you hear news of a privately-owned company making the transition to public trading through an initial public offering (IPO). In essence, this is the act of selling your shares to any member of the public who wishes to buy, which can seem like an attractive alternative to selling your business to an individual.

Realistically, taking a company public is not a practical exit strategy, because very few companies have the characteristics necessary to be successful on Wall Street. Analysts measure every detail of a company's finances, along with prospects for profit, growth, and expansion. The few businesses that succeed with an IPO are already very profitable, or there is a strong likelihood of massive future growth. If you decide to pursue this type of sale, getting professional investors on board early is key. These individuals have experience with taking companies public, making it more likely that your business will succeed in this endeavor.

If you choose to bring professional investors in, remember that you are doing so in exchange for some of your ownership interest in the company. As a result, going public may not offer the financial boost you expect. It is also critical to keep an eye on Wall Street analysts and make recommended changes as appropriate. For many business owners, this is a chore that takes away from core leadership functions. Finally, bear in mind that there are costs associated with the transition from privately-owned to publicly-traded. For example, underwriting fees can reduce your profit from the IPO.

The tax ramifications of an IPO require specialized knowledge and skills, so it is wise to consult your Certified Tax Coach to avoid any wrong turns in the maze.

Everything Must Go

When selling the company isn't a viable option and giving it away doesn't make sense, some business owners elect to liquidate when they are ready to change careers or retire. While this is certainly the simplest way to separate yourself from the business, it doesn't offer you much in the way of financial benefits. While you can sell the company's tangible assets, you won't get a penny for the work you put into building your client base. After liquidating all of the items you can, the proceeds must first go to paying any outstanding business debts. When all of the creditors are satisfied, anything left over can be divided among the company's owners. Most people faced with a need to leave their company choose liquidation as a last resort, due to the high probability that closing the business will leave them with nothing to show for years of work.

Leveraging Employee Stock Ownership Plans (ESOP)

One of the most effective—but least utilized—methods of transferring ownership of a business is the Employee Stock Ownership Plan (ESOP). These programs offer tax advantages that other succession planning tools do not, making them an appealing option for a seamless transition when you leave the organization.

In essence, ESOPs are programs that give or sell shares of the company to staff members as part of a larger compensation program. ESOPs are designed to reduce or eliminate shareholder taxes, so that employees are motivated to invest in the business. Some organizations allow all staff members to participate, but for succession planning purposes, participation might be limited. For example, ESOP shareholders could be partners in the business who want to buy a departing peer out, but simply cannot afford to do so outright.

ESOPs are created when the business designates a trust to acquire and hold company stock on behalf of participating employees. In some cases, organizations borrow money from their financial institutions to fund the purchase of new or existing stock, and the subsequent contributions of stock to the trust are tax deductible.

After the trust is established, stock is transferred to employees according to a formula pre-determined by the organization. Many companies choose vesting schedules based on seniority, so the longer an employee works for the organization, the closer he gets to having full ownership of the stock. Employees who are fully vested in an ESOP have the option of selling their shares back to the business at fair market value once they are ready to leave the company.

The tax benefits of an ESOP make this an attractive option for business owners, as well as employees. Examples include:

- Stock contributions made by the business are generally tax deductible.

- Organizations that take a loan from their financial institution to purchase the stock may be able to deduct some or all of the loan payments.

- Profits of companies that are structured as S Corporations pass to individuals for tax purposes. However, the ESOP trust is considered a tax-exempt shareholder, which reduces the tax burden on individuals.

- Employee contributions to an ESOP are not taxed until a disbursement is issued.

- Employees can roll distributions into their IRAs or investment accounts, in which case they are taxed under capital gains regulations.

Business owners who are ready to leave the organization can leverage the power of their company's ESOP to simplify the process of selling ownership shares. Instead of working to secure a buyer who is interested in purchasing the shares—and has the means to do so—shares can be sold to the ESOP trust.

Of course, ESOPs are not right for every business. Your Certified Tax Coach may recommend against such programs for one of the following reasons:

- Companies must be structured as S Corporations or C Corporations to participate in an ESOP program.
- Setting up an ESOP may be costly.
- Adding new shares for the purpose of creating an ESOP can dilute the value of existing shares.

Finally, when it comes to relying on an ESOP as your exit strategy, there is an important caveat: the company must be financially prepared to purchase your shares when they are sold to the ESOP. Smaller organizations might find this challenging, in which case you must have an alternative option for leaving the business.

While an ESOP may not be the solution for every organization, some closely held private corporations are using this method with great success. Consult your Certified Tax Coach and your financial advisor to determine whether an ESOP is right for you and your company.

The Role of Insurance in Succession Planning

Insurance is specifically designed to protect against unexpected or unusual events, and the loss of a company's owner certainly qualifies. Key Person Insurance can be targeted for use in succession planning, as it protects against an unplanned departure due to the death of an owner or key employee.

Most business owners have life insurance policies to protect their families if they pass away unexpectedly. Life insurance replaces lost household income to ensure that dependents can afford their living expenses when an important source of income is gone. Key Person Insurance is built on a similar concept, except it is the business that is protected, receiving financial support if a critical staff member passes away. In a small business, this is usually the owner, the founder, or perhaps a key employee or two. If the company loses an employee that is crucial to the business, the life or death of the company is on the line as well. But if a key person unexpectedly dies and the company is protected with Key Person Insurance, the company receives the insurance payoff, allowing it to keep running. The company pays the premiums for such plans and receives related benefits. This can be particularly important if the business is in the process of being sold, as many of these transactions take place over time. Those selling a business may choose to take a Key Person Insurance policy on the buyer, and the buyer may want a policy on the seller. If the buyer dies, the seller is protected from sudden disruption to the business that impacts any outstanding payments. If the seller dies, the buyer can make any remaining payments to simplify the situation for the seller's beneficiaries.

Protecting Your Wealth

Some entrepreneurs build their businesses with the intention of selling after a few years. Others make careers out of their companies, dedicating decades to the organization's success. Either way, it takes an extraordinary amount of planning and countless hours of work to transform an idea into a full-fledged business. Without a carefully planned exit strategy, all of that work can be lost.

Protect your investment of time and resources by carefully considering your exit strategy. The earlier you start thinking about your eventual exit from the organization, the more effective your plan will work to protect your wealth. Your Certified Tax Coach and financial planning specialist can walk you through the maze of this process, so that you choose the best strategy for you. Whether you sell the company to the highest bidder or gift it to a family member, creating a plan today can ensure that you are well-positioned to save on taxes when the time comes to make your exit.

ABOUT THE AUTHOR

David Auer, CPA, MS, PFS, CGMA, JD, LLM in Taxation

With over 30 years of experience, David Auer is the Founder and CEO of Provident CPAs. David earned his BSBA and MS in Accounting from Oklahoma State University, his JD with honors from Oklahoma University College of Law, and his LLM in Taxation from New York University School of Law. He has the Personal Financial Specialist (PFS) and Chartered Global Management Accountant (CGMA) designations with the American Institute of CPAs. David is a Fellow with the Esperti Peterson Institute and member of the Order of the Coif, Wealth Counsel, The American Association of Attorneys-CPAs, and The National Academy of Best Selling Authors.

David is a frequent speaker, is recognized as one of America's Premier Experts®, is on the adjunct faculty of Asset Protection Corporation founded by internationally acclaimed asset protection attorney Robert Lambert, LLM in Taxation, Esq., and is the author or co-author of several books, including 57 Ways to Grow Your Business – Bright Ideas for Serious Entrepreneurs; "You Can Deduct THAT?"; 10 Most Expensive Tax Mistakes That Cost Business Owners Thousands; and Ignite Your Life with Brian Tracy; Performance 360 Special Edition with Richard Branson; and The Road to Success with Jack Canfield.

Mr. Auer no longer practices law and focuses solely on consulting, writing, speaking, and tax planning as a CPA, Business Advisor, and Outsourced CFO for his clients. If you would like to learn more about how he can help you lower your taxes, increase business profits, and create and protect your wealth, please email david.auer@providentcpas.com or call 1-85-LOWER-TAX.

CHAPTER 12

Setting the Course: Planning Ahead for the End of the Maze

BY JOSEPH REYES, CPA, CTC

Though it may seem counterintuitive, your tax obligations do not end after your death. In fact, without careful planning, all of the tax savings strategies you employed along the way can vanish, and your estate could be saddled with a significant tax bill. The regulations around estate taxes are extremely complicated, making it difficult to navigate through them on your own. Protecting your wealth requires help from a skilled guide, such as a Certified Tax Coach. These are a few of the most important tax landmarks to be aware of regarding your estate.

The Twists and Turns of Estate Taxes

The taxes you pay on your income are in an entirely separate class when compared to the taxes you are responsible for after you pass away. They are also in a separate category from probate expenses, which are fees associated with managing your estate if you die without a will or a revocable living trust. Estate taxes are federal taxes levied on the net value of your estate before any funds are distributed to your beneficiaries. Specifically, according to the IRS, you are taxed on your right to transfer your property to others when you die. This is in addition to any generation-skipping taxes, which may be applicable to gifts left to your grandchildren.

One of the most alarming issues that crop up for beneficiaries—and the one you most want to avoid through careful planning—is that taxes must be paid in full within nine months of your death. If your estate and your beneficiaries don't have the necessary amount of cash, it may become necessary to sell assets to pay the tax bill. This is a common occurrence when assets include real estate or interests in a business. It can be heartbreaking when this situation leads to the dissolution of a family business or the sale of a family homestead.

The good news is that there is no estate tax on wealth that is transferred to your spouse, as long as your marriage is recognized in the United States, and your spouse is a US citizen. This does not include registered domestic partnerships, civil unions, and similar arrangements. For some, this exemption alone solves the estate tax problem. However, most people have additional plans for a portion of their estate—whether or not they are married—which makes planning ahead a priority.

The Impact of Taxes on Your Estate

The first step in a comprehensive plan to minimize estate taxes is to gain a clear understanding of whether estate regulations are likely to apply to you. However, this isn't quite as straightforward as it seems. There are layers to the labyrinth, with exemptions for estates that are valued under a certain amount, but the amount changes regularly through congressional action.

For example, in 2013, your estate was only liable for taxes if it was valued at more than $5,250,000. In 2014, that amount increased to $5,340,000. Subsequent years brought additional increases in the threshold: $5,430,000 (2015), $5,450,000 (2016), $5,490,000 (2017), and finally settled on $11.2 million in 2018. The estate tax rate has remained consistent at 40 percent since 2013, however it fluctuated dramatically in preceding years. Predicting how estate taxes will change between now and the end of your life is a challenge. In addition, the large increase beginning in 2018 will last only until 2026, when the thresholds will revert back.

Adding to the complexity, there may be death or inheritance taxes assessed at the state level. It is entirely possible that your estate will be exempt from federal taxes but still be liable for state taxes. An experienced tax advisor or Certified Tax Coach will assist you in designing a plan to minimize both.

Calculating the Value of Your Estate

Creating a plan to reduce your tax liability requires a clear understanding of how the value of your estate is calculated. Because your wealth may consist of many different assets, the gross value of your estate is based on the fair market value of each item. Examples of assets included in the calculation of your estate's value include cash, securities, trusts, annuities, insurance, real estate, and business interests. Anything of value should be included in the calculation, even personal items. Fine jewelry, certain items of clothing, and antique furniture are examples of assets that are commonly overlooked.

Certain deductions reduce the total value of your estate, such as mortgages, estate administration expenses, certain charitable contributions, and wealth that is transferred to your surviving spouse. Costs related to your funeral can also be deducted. The remaining value of your estate, once the applicable deductions are taken, is the amount to be taxed.

Three Strategies for Reducing Estate Taxes

There are a variety of strategies for minimizing your tax liability when you exit the maze, but three stand out because they are highly effective. Begin your journey by determining whether these strategies apply to you and if so, how. After exploring these three options, work through those that are less common.

Combining Exemptions

Because there are no estate taxes assessed on wealth transferred to your spouse after your death, this is a good starting point for creating a comprehensive tax minimization plan. You can virtually eliminate estate taxes after your death. However, it is unwise to rely on this strategy exclusively, as estate taxes will apply to the estate of your spouse at the time of his or her death.

When the surviving spouse passes away, the current estate exemption applies ($11.2 million in 2018). In addition, any exemption that was not used by the first spouse can be applied to the second spouse's estate. This was made effective in 2013. The ability to use a deceased spouse's remaining exemption amount is referred to as "portability." Theoretically, this can result in complete exemption for an estate valued under $24,399,000 in 2018. However, there is a catch: the second spouse cannot use exemptions remaining from the first spouse if he or she remarries. This is a possibility to consider during the estate planning process.

This estate planning method is based on what essentially amounts to spouses leaving their entire accumulated wealth to each other. It is important to note that if this strategy is implemented without a detailed plan, the first spouse to die has virtually no control over how the funds are used during the surviving spouse's lifetime, and the surviving spouse can make most of the decisions about how funds will be distributed once he or she also dies.

If this is an issue for either spouse, there are steps that can be taken to ensure that each person's wishes are followed after death. Your financial advisor, tax professional, or Certified Tax Coach may suggest splitting your estate into two separate trusts, which allows each of you to use your full exemption and reduce your taxable estate. Through these trusts, you can still pass a significant portion of your estate to other family members. Typically, such trusts are set up in a way that allows either spouse to access the assets in either trust, while still separating assets to take advantage of both estate tax exemptions. For most married couples, this is the simplest and most efficient method of minimizing estate taxes.

Transferring Your Wealth During Your Lifetime

Estate taxes are calculated based on the net value of your assets at the time of your death, so a common method of minimizing estate taxes is to reduce your assets before you die. One of the most popular ways to do this is through gifts to your loved ones and future beneficiaries throughout your lifetime. Tax benefits aside, it can be extraordinarily rewarding to see the results of such gifts for yourself. You can enjoy visiting family members in homes you helped purchase and you can watch with pride as grandchildren walk across the graduation stage thanks to an education you helped fund.

There are taxes associated with gift giving, and the annual exemption amount is much lower than for estate taxes. Again, these exemptions are regularly reviewed by Congress, and they are subject to change. Since 2014, the amount that qualifies for exemption is $14,000 per year and finally increased to $15,000 beginning in 2018. Note that married couples can double this, as each spouse is entitled to make $15,000 gifts, and the $15,000 exemption is per recipient. If you have several grandchildren, you and your spouse can give each of them $15,000 per year without paying gift taxes, and gifts can be made to anyone, not just family members. Over time, these smaller amounts can add up, removing a significant portion of the assets from your estate by the time you pass away.

Staying under the $15,000 gift tax exemption isn't always practical, particularly when there are time constraints on your part or the recipient(s) have significant financial needs. If you go over the $15,000 limit, you are responsible for paying gift taxes under most circumstances, and the amount over the $15,000 limit reduces the exemption available for your estate. Tax rates for gifts over the exempted amount match the tax rates for estates. However, there are important exceptions to the gift tax exemption limit that can enhance your ability to transfer significant funds. As long as you pay providers directly, you are not taxed and there is no limit to the amount you spend on tuition, medical, and dental expenses. This applies to anyone you wish to supply tuition or medical treatment for, not just family members.

While cash is a common choice for gift-giving, other assets can be gifted through this process. In some cases, you can achieve better results from a tax savings perspective by gifting non-cash assets. This is primarily true of assets that are expected to appreciate, and in particular, assets that will appreciate quite a bit, as both the original gift and the value of the appreciation do not become part of your estate.

If you choose to gift non-cash assets, be aware that the recipient is still impacted by your cost basis. If recipients eventually sell the assets, they may be subject to capital gains taxes for the difference between what you originally paid and the eventual sales price. Still, capital gains taxes are substantially lower than estate taxes, so the end result is a lower tax bill for those who stand to inherit your wealth.

Finally, charitable gifts are typically exempt from taxes, and the limits are quite high. You can donate up to 50 percent of your adjusted gross income to public charities, private operating foundations, and certain private foundations each year, reducing your tax liability significantly.

Creating Trusts to Reduce Tax Liability

There are a variety of trusts intended to meet all sorts of needs, from setting funds aside for a loved one's future medical expenses to creating ongoing income for your beneficiaries after your death. One of the most important differences between trusts is whether they are set up as "revocable" or "irrevocable." When you create a revocable trust, you can change your mind about the trust and any assets in it at any time. However, an irrevocable trust is a permanent decision. Once you assign assets to an irrevocable trust, that trust is the permanent owner. Revocable versus irrevocable becomes important when creating your long-term estate planning strategy.

Irrevocable Life Insurance Trust (ILIT)

If you wish to avoid estate taxes on the death benefits of your life insurance policy, an Irrevocable Life Insurance Trust (ILIT) can provide a simple solution. Once your attorney sets up the trust, you transfer ownership of your life insurance policy to the trust. As long as this is done three or more years before the end of your life, death benefits belong to the trust and they are not included in your estate for tax purposes.

Your ILIT becomes the beneficiary of your life insurance policy, which opens up a vast array of options when it comes to distributing the funds. There is no need for your death benefits to be removed from the ILIT right away, giving you an opportunity to create a disbursement schedule according to your preferences. Most people use this feature to pass funds to beneficiaries over time, removing the risk that young or irresponsible beneficiaries will mismanage their inheritance. The specifics of when and how beneficiaries are able to access funds are virtually unlimited. Some people create trusts that disperse regular periodic payments, while others transfer the funds when beneficiaries reach a particular milestone, for example a certain age, the birth of a child, completion of higher education, and so on.

Qualified Personal Residence Trust

Another common trust for estate planning purposes is the Qualified Personal Residence Trust (QPRT). Essentially you set up the QPRT and transfer ownership of your home to the trust for a period of time, typically ten to fifteen years. During this period, you continue to live in the home, and afterwards, ownership passes to the beneficiaries of your trust without becoming part of your estate for tax purposes.

The benefits of a QPRT are related to how the value of the gift is calculated. In simple terms, transferring ownership of the home to a trust reduces the taxable value of the asset. Because you will continue to live in the home, its value is reduced for gift tax purposes. The main caveat to realizing these benefits is that you must outlive the trust term, so it is important to consider related factors when creating the trust.

Grantor Retained Annuity Trust

While a QPRT must be used exclusively for your home, there are similar options for other types of assets. One of the most commonly used is the Grantor Retained Annuity Trust (GRAT). After setting up a GRAT, you can transfer ownership of income-generating assets.

Examples include businesses, stocks, and real estate. You pay a tax when the trust is established and you will continue to receive the income, but the asset is effectively removed from your estate for tax purposes.

GRATs are appropriate for assets that generate consistent income. If you have assets that generate variable income, your financial services professional is likely to recommend a Grantor Retained UniTrust (GRUT). A GRUT is another irrevocable trust where the grantor retains the right to receive funds annually from the trust based on a fixed percentage that is recalculated annually based on the new value of the trust. In either case, these irrevocable trusts are effective for a specified period, after which assets are transferred to your beneficiaries. If you do not outlive the term of the trust, assets may be included in your estate.

Family Limited Partnership or LLC

After a lifetime of building your wealth with a family farm, business, or property, the last thing you want is to lose some of its value to estate taxes. Fortunately, there is a solution to protect family assets. A Family Limited Partnership (FLP) or Family LLC (FLLC) offers tax benefits as well as critical protections. For example, an FLP or FLLC shields these assets from creditors and lawsuits, ensuring that they won't be lost due to unforeseen and unintended circumstances. Better still, you retain some control over the farm, business, or real estate.

As with QPRTs and GRATs, you begin by setting up the entity, then ownership of assets is transferred. You are then issued ownership interests in the FLP or FLLC. You continue to control the FLP as a general partner or the FLLC as a manager, though you may have new fiduciary obligations to the other owners. If you choose to give your ownership interests to your children, their value is no longer part of your estate. You still have veto power when it comes to whether your children sell or transfer the ownership shares, so there is no risk of losing your farm, business, or property due to their mismanagement. Finally, there is an additional tax benefit to this strategy in that the value of ownership shares is typically quite low, simply because there is no market for these interests.

Charitable Remainder Trust

The Charitable Remainder Trust (CRT) offers tax savings in several areas, while simultaneously giving you an opportunity to financially support the charitable causes that are most important to you. While these trusts operate in a similar manner to the others already discussed, CRTs are exclusively designed to benefit tax-exempt organizations.

Once you have created a CRT you transfer assets into it, just as you would with other types of trusts. Generally, the best assets to transfer are those that are likely to appreciate significantly. You will benefit by retaining lifetime income from these assets, while avoiding capital gains taxes when the asset is sold. In addition, you realize an immediate tax deduction at the time of the transfer, and the asset is no longer considered part of your estate.

This trust includes an option to sell assets at some future point, and the sale is made at market value. However, the trust pays no capital gains taxes, and proceeds are typically reinvested in income-producing assets. As a result of this strategy, you receive income from the trust, and because the principal is not reduced by capital gains taxes, your income will be higher than it would have been otherwise. When you do eventually pass away, the assets in your CRT are transferred to the charity you selected.

As you journey through the tax maze, some of the twists and turns present unique challenges. Creating a comprehensive plan to protect your wealth from high estate taxes is one of the biggest challenges of all. After a lifetime of working to build a legacy, losing almost half of your estate to tax collectors is disappointing to say the least. Fortunately, your financial services providers and your Certified Tax Coach can guide you through this particular area of the maze by designing a customized strategy to minimize the tax obligations of your estate.

By planning ahead and taking advantage of a variety of options, you can maximize your use of the estate tax exemption. In addition, you can create a gift-giving strategy that reduces the size of your estate, while also allowing you the joy of seeing the results firsthand. Finally, strategic placement of assets in a variety of irrevocable trusts ensures your beneficiaries receive the greatest benefit. Don't make your way through the labyrinth alone. Consult a Certified Tax Coach to begin estate planning right away.

Sources

- https://www.irs.gov/businesses/small-businesses-self-employed/estate-tax
- https://www.irs.gov/businesses/small-businesses-self-employed/frequently-asked-questions-on-estate-taxes#18
- https://www.irs.gov/businesses/small-businesses-self-employed/gift-tax
- https://www.irs.gov/businesses/small-businesses-self-employed/frequently-asked-questions-on-gift-taxes
- https://www.forbes.com/sites/ashleaebeling/2016/10/25/irs-announces-2017-estate-and-gift-tax-limits-the-11-million-tax-break/#43a6dd853b70
- https://www.irs.gov/charities-non-profits/charitable-organizations/charitable-contribution-deductions

Joseph L. Reyes, CPA, CTC

Joseph L. Reyes is a Certified Public Accountant and Certified Management Accountant with a Master of Science in Finance. Add to that his designation as a Certified Tax Coach and he has all the qualifications necessary to help business owners manage their finances and save big money on their tax bills. Joseph is also a Registered Representative of H.D. Vest and is well positioned to assist business owners in setting up retirement accounts, doing financial planning, and helping build wealth. He offers a comprehensive service to deal with most financial issues small businesses face. He insists on proactive planning as the key to being tax efficient and financially ahead of the curve.

JL Reyes Tax Planning

North Wales, Pennsylvania 19454

.

CHAPTER 13

Tax ID Theft: When Every Path Is Blocked

BY DREW FOSTER, EA

Security breaches impact millions of consumers each year, putting their sensitive personal information in the hands of thieves and cybercriminals. One of the worst incidents occurred in 2017, when the credit reporting bureau Equifax announced that more than 145 million customers' names, social security numbers, and dates of birth had been stolen.

Loss of this sort of information exposes impacted individuals to identity theft and tax ID theft, with potentially devastating results. If you are a victim, it can feel like every path in the tax maze is blocked as you try to repair the damage and correct your records. Fortunately, the IRS has made preventing and addressing tax ID theft a priority. That means help is available if you discover your data has been compromised. Your Certified Tax Coach is an excellent resource when it comes to restoring your identity.

Refund Fraud Basics

One of the most common issues that the IRS comes across is tax refund fraud, which cost the US Treasury almost $6 billion in 2016. There are two types of tax refund fraud that occur quite frequently. These are investigated carefully by IRS Criminal Investigators through the Questionable Refund Program (QRP) and the Return Preparer Program (RPP).

Tax refund fraud involves situations in which tax returns are filed using false information and statements with the intent of getting access to unearned tax refunds. Typically, these returns are not filed by real taxpayers. Instead, criminals use other peoples' personal data to file returns claiming false refundable federal tax credits or false income tax withholdings to get cash payments they aren't entitled to. Examples of refundable tax credits include the Earned Income Tax Credit, part of the American Opportunity Tax Credit, and the Small Business Health Care Tax Credit. In certain cases, licensed return preparers are responsible for these crimes on a large scale, filing false income tax returns using many taxpayers' information.

The IRS Criminal Investigator Division takes these concerns seriously, and there are four Scheme Development Centers (SDCs) that are fully focused on detecting tax refund fraud. They have been quite successful, shutting down many a QRP and RPP plot. An entire SDC is specifically dedicated to identity theft refund fraud, working hard to protect you from those trying to use your personal information in their theft.

The good news is that the IRS is quite skilled in catching and putting tax ID thieves away, and it is unusual for criminals to get away with refund fraud long-term. However, the disruption that comes with tax ID theft isn't always solved when the criminals are caught. The IRS and your Certified Tax Coach can help you put the pieces back together again.

Common Tax ID Scams

Tax ID theft comes in a variety of forms, and the goal is almost always to steal information needed to file a fraudulent tax return. The IRS Criminal Investigator Division has identified some of the most common tax ID scams.

- **Fraudulent Refunds by Prisoners** – The biggest year for fraudulent refunds to prisoners was 2012. During that tax season, more than 110,000 prisoners filed false returns claiming they were owed approximately $1 billion. Typically, the scheme involved filing returns using information stolen from other prisoners, but there were a number of variations. This issue has decreased in recent years, but there are still regular incidents of fraudulent prisoner returns.

- **Stolen Dependents** – In an effort to claim additional Earned Income Credit refunds, tax ID thieves will target children's information. They claim these children as dependents on their own returns, increasing the amount of their cash refund.

- **Tax ID Theft by Prior Year Preparer** – When you hire a tax preparer to manage your returns, you have no choice but to provide your personal information. Unfortunately, some tax preparers aren't who they seem. There have been cases where these individuals use former clients' data to file fraudulent returns.

- **Tax ID Theft from Individuals Unlikely to File a Return** – There are a number of reasons why people are not required to file federal tax returns. One of the most common is low levels of income. For example, in 2016, individuals who were under the age of 65 and single did not have to file a tax return if their income was less than $10,350. Thieves steal tax identification information from individuals that appear to fit these criteria, then they file fraudulent returns claiming refunds.

All of these scams rely on a criminal's ability to steal your tax ID data, and the methods of gaining access to your information have gotten more and more creative.

Common Strategies for Stealing Your Information

There are many ways that criminals steal your personal information. Some are technologically sophisticated, while others are more rudimentary. While you can't always keep your data safe, understanding how thieves operate can help you protect against basic identity theft tactics.

Dumpster Diving – Keeping a shredder in your home can thwart one of the oldest methods of identity theft, often referred to as dumpster diving. As the name suggests, criminals go through your trash to get ahold of discarded paperwork such as credit card bills, utility bills, bank statements, and health insurance records. They use the details on these documents to steal your identity, filing fraudulent tax returns or applying for credit in your name. Cross-cut shredders are a great way to keep your personal information safe. Alternatively, you may wish to consider switching to online and email statements.

Mail Theft – Though it is a bit riskier than dumpster diving, identity thieves have been known to steal sensitive documents right out of the mail. Some keep an eye on your mailbox and pull important information out before you even see it, while others reroute your mail entirely using the post office's change of address procedure. In addition to using online and email services to get your bills, you can protect against mail theft by taking your mail out immediately, investing in a mailbox with a lock, or renting a mailbox at the post office. If you notice missing items, contact your local post office immediately for more information on next steps.

Social Engineering and Pretexting – Though this method of stealing personal data is usually directed at businesses, anyone can fall victim to social engineering and pretexting. Con artists develop convincing schemes to persuade you that they are calling from your human resources department, a government agency, or technical support, and once they gain your trust, they exploit it to get cash, passwords, bank information, and/or tax identification details. In one elaborate scheme, thieves call you pretending to be IRS agents, and they tell you that you will be arrested if you don't wire money to pay an old tax debt. The callers are convincing, as they already have enough personal details about you to appear legitimate. Before you know it, you have sent an untraceable money transfer for an IRS debt you didn't owe.

Protecting yourself against social engineering and pretexting starts with refusing to let any caller or emailer rush you into sharing personal information or sending money. To be effective, these criminals try hard to pressure you into immediate action before you have time to think the situation through. Take a moment to locate a legitimate callback number and verify the caller's claims, or to do a quick online search for common schemes. For example, the IRS pretext is pretty well-known, and the IRS website clearly states that you will never receive a call demanding immediate payment and threatening arrest.

Shoulder Surfing – When someone stands too close to you while you are checking out at the register, they could have more on their mind than simply invading your personal space. Shoulder surfing is a technique in which experienced criminals peek at your PIN number while you enter it into register keypads or ATM machines. If they can also see your card number—or steal the card itself—they can use the information to steal from your account. This same method is used to gain access to other sensitive information, for example your social security number or your date of birth. By positioning themselves at the right place and time, thieves can casually get ahold of your personal data. It is important to note that you don't actually see some shoulder surfers at all. These individuals have access to security cameras, and they watch the footage to see what you write or type.

Protect your information by positioning yourself to block the view of any onlookers or cameras when typing your PIN or other details. If this isn't possible, let the other person in line go first, or skip the transaction altogether. Remember, these sorts of criminals don't expect to be successful every time, and if you make it even a little difficult to see your information, they will move on to the next potential victim.

Purse and Wallet Theft – Perhaps the most well-known method of identity theft is stealing your purse or wallet. Most people carry a lot of detailed personal information with them including cell phones, photo identification, blank checks, health insurance ID cards, and credit cards. If you purse or wallet is stolen, notify your financial institutions right away to prevent your information from being used to drain your bank account. Prevention is the best way to mitigate this risk. Keep an eye on your things and consider carrying the bare minimum you need to get through the day. If you don't have to carry all of your cards or you can get rid of old receipts and deposit slips, there is less for thieves to work with.

Credit and Debit Card Theft – Credit and debit card thieves have come a long way since the days when they stole your actual cards. Today's criminals can gain access to your account when you make purchases through unverified websites, or they use "skimmers" to copy your card information for use elsewhere. Chip cards and verification codes are making it harder to use credit card numbers fraudulently, but every time financial institutions get one step ahead, criminals find a new way to steal. Consider using payment services that make it possible to buy online without entering your card numbers. You can also use a pre-paid card when you aren't certain about security, so that there are limited funds to steal if something goes wrong.

Phishing – Cybercriminals have mastered the art of disguising their attempts to steal personal data in legitimate looking emails. Whether they trick you into clicking on a link or downloading dangerous software, these techniques make it possible for the sender to use your identity for credit applications or tax fraud. The first line of defense is to delete any emails you weren't expecting. If there appears to be a critical issue, call the sender directly instead of opening attachments, clicking links, or replying with personal details. Your financial institution will never ask you to divulge your user ID and password and the IRS will never request that you provide your social security number, so if you receive requests like this, you know there is a scam.

Because so many people are aware of the dangers that come with opening and downloading unfamiliar attachments and files, cybercriminals are using these methods less frequently. Instead, they persuade you to click on a link that takes you to a site which looks very much like your financial institution. However, if you check the actual web address, you will see that something isn't right. Instead of an address that starts with www.yourfinancialinstitution.com, you will see www.nonsensewords.yourfinancialinstitution.com. This is an indication that the link is a scam, intended to trick you into entering your user ID and password.

When in doubt, call the sender directly, or close the message and type the agency or institution's web address into your browser. Reputable agencies and businesses understand the need for caution when it comes to sharing personal information, and they will work with you to resolve issues in the most secure manner possible.

There are dozens of variations on all of these methods, and criminals are constantly inventing new ways to access your personal data. While you can't do much about thieves who break into corporate databases, you can protect yourself from some of the more basic identity theft tactics. If you do become a victim of identity theft or tax fraud, there are resources that can help you navigate the many twists and turns that come with getting your records corrected. You can also rest assured that major government agencies, including the IRS and the FBI, have entire investigation units dedicated to tax ID and identity theft.

Obstacles Facing the IRS

While you are focused on minimizing your tax liability, the IRS has separate goals. The agency's mission statement is to "provide America's taxpayers top quality service by helping them understand and meet their tax responsibilities and by applying the tax law with integrity and fairness to all." Unfortunately, there are significant challenges to achieving this goal.

First, tax ID theft undermines the entire process, requiring the agency to devote significant resources to preventing and investigating fraud. There are millions of these incidents occurring every year, which overwhelms units tasked with maintaining the integrity of the process. Second, in part because of the need to invest time and money into fraud prevention, there simply aren't enough resources to provide excellent service to all of the taxpayers who need help. Getting through to a representative by phone can take hours, and mail correspondence often means months of waiting.

The digital transformation has been slow in reaching the IRS, but some digital features are now in place. The agency offers online transcript services, digital payment solutions, and the ability for taxpayers to complete common requests, such as payment plans, right online. These tools mean significant savings for the agency. By some estimates, managing a single customer call can cost more than $42, while the same transaction completed online costs the agency less than 25 cents.

Using high-quality digital security measures, taxpayers can safely manage some of their tax-related tasks digitally, freeing up agency resources for more careful monitoring of tax ID theft and fraudulent returns. You can help the IRS protect your information by taking a few simple steps.

IRS Recommendations for Protecting Your Tax ID

While it isn't possible to remove all risk of tax ID theft, you can minimize the chances of becoming a victim. Begin by diligently protecting your personal identification information and your financial records. Use a cross-cut shredder to dispose of sensitive documents, and avoid carrying your social security card in your purse or wallet. There are very few reasons why you should need to give your social security number to anyone, so carefully research the legitimacy of any requests you receive.

Your personal information is often stored on your electronic devices, including laptops and mobile phones. Use strong passwords to prevent others from accessing your information. Protect data on your computer with anti-spam and anti-virus software and a firewall. A firewall is a hardware and/or software program that acts as a barrier to keep destructive elements out of a network or specific computer; it prevents unauthorized user access. This technology keeps criminals from hacking into your computer to view your personal details.

Saving passwords and payment information in online services is a common habit, but it isn't always safe. You can't always be sure how a company is protecting your saved information, and you could be at risk if the site is breached. Think twice about saving sensitive data online, and change your passwords frequently for your online accounts. When two-factor authentication is available, take advantage of the extra layer of protection.

Most important, be aware that the IRS will not contact you through phone, text message, or social media. If there is an issue, you will receive a letter in the mail. Finally, if you are aware of any suspicious activity, report it directly to the IRS. For example, you might notice that your tax preparer uses unorthodox methods to complete your returns. Visit IRS.gov for more information on reporting suspected fraud.

When You Are A Victim

The first sign that someone has stolen your information for tax fraud usually comes in the form of a letter from the IRS stating that a tax return has already been filed under your tax ID. This letter may come if you try to e-file and your return is rejected. If you fall victim to a tax ID scam, the IRS has tools and resources available to help you.

Begin by filing a report with the FTC at identitytheft.gov, then contact the three major credit bureaus to place a fraud alert on your credit records. Contact information for the credit bureaus is as follows:

- Equifax – www.Equifax.com 1-888-766-0008
- Experian – www.Experian.com 1-888-397-3742
- TransUnion – www.TransUnion.com 1-800-680-7289

Examine your credit reports from all three bureaus and immediately close any fraudulent accounts.

Respond to the IRS letter using the contact information provided. You will probably be required to complete IRS Form 14039 – Identity Theft Affidavit. Attach this form to your paper return, and mail it into the IRS. Going forward, the IRS may issue you an IP PIN, which is a six-digit number that you can use to e-file. If so, you will receive a new IP PIN by mail every year to prevent future fraudulent returns. You can learn more about IRS programs to support victims of tax ID theft at IRS.gov/identitytheft.

Tax ID theft is a lucrative crime, making people and businesses attractive targets for thieves and cybercriminals. Unfortunately, it is all too common to be a victim of identity theft or tax ID theft in one form or another. By taking common sense precautions, you can minimize your risk. As aforementioned, you can verify that callers, email senders, and websites are legitimate before you give them any personal information. And if you do discover that your tax ID has been stolen, don't despair. There are tools and resources available to help you. The IRS has customer service agents that specialize in managing tax ID theft issues, and there are procedures in place to get you back on track as quickly as possible. Your Certified Tax Coach can also assist in sorting out any obstacles you face as a result of tax ID theft and will help you get out of the maze intact.

ABOUT THE AUTHOR

Drew Foster, EA

Drew Foster cofounded IRS Solutions, an IRS Tax Resolution Software. As an Enrolled Agent, Drew has helped hundreds of clients navigate the IRS. Drew decided to help give other tax professionals the tools they need to help their clients deal with the IRS. Cofounding IRS Solutions with David Stone, who worked for the IRS for 12 years, they created IRS Solutions Tax Resolution Software.

Drew Foster's tax planning firm takes financial strategy beyond mere tax preparation. As a Certified Tax Coach, Mr. Foster brings clients' tax plans to a higher level of efficiency. Working together with Certified Tax Coach David Stone, Mr. Foster assists in saving clients saving as much as $50,000 per year. His history in the financial services industry includes several awards that recognize his ability to help companies exceed their profit goals.

Founded on his extensive knowledge of this industry, Mr. Foster's tax strategies routinely save his clients $15,000 in the first year of planning together. With the ongoing education and specialized training requisite to his licensing as a Certified Tax Coach, his financial guidance proves invaluable to clients seeking an effective means of reducing tax and achieving greater profits.

Mr. Foster has a habit of excelling wherever he goes. As a high school football player, he broke the school record for most receiving yards in a game. After college, he led his branch of US Bank from one of the lowest performing rates to one of the highest in just one year. In a later position, he was awarded the "40 under 40" award, as one of a select number of local young professionals making significant achievements in their business and community.

IRS Solutions is located in Valencia, California, and Drew can be contacted online at www.irssolutions.com or by phone at (661) 775-6200.

CHAPTER 14

Hitting a Wall: What to Do When You Can't Pay

BY DAVID STONE, EA

Despite careful planning and implementation of a comprehensive tax minimization strategy, many people learn that they still owe taxes when it comes time to file their returns. If you're lucky, the bill is low enough for you to pay easily. Unfortunately, that's not always the case. If you have hit a wall in the tax labyrinth and you can't pay the amount you owe by April 15th, don't worry; there are plenty of options. The most important thing to remember is that doing nothing is a dead-end path. You will inevitably find yourself owing much more than you otherwise would have, and you will certainly have to pay at least the full amount sooner or later.

Common Reasons for an Inability to Pay

Individuals often find themselves unable to pay their taxes on time when they run into an unusual and unexpectedly high tax bill. There are several common reasons this occurs:

- **New Self-Employment Income** – When you first start out with self-employment, it can be tough to understand the tax implications. Often, filing after your first year as an entrepreneur brings unpleasant surprises.

- **Incorrect W-4 Withholding** – Whether you deliberately had the least amount possible withheld to increase your take-home pay or you miscalculated when you completed your W-4, incorrect withholdings are a common reason for unexpectedly high tax bills.
- **One-time Windfall** – Major life events like a death in the family or a divorce can result in a one-time influx of cash. Unfortunately, the related tax liability can be a shock.

Businesses face a separate set of issues that can lead to large tax bills. A slowdown in sales or a decline in the economy can disrupt cash flow significantly. In some cases, business owners must choose between paying employees and paying taxes. While paying employees is critical on many levels, failure to pay taxes leads to its own set of problems.

No matter what the circumstances, consider asking a professional to review your taxes. Certified Tax Coaches, tax attorneys, and accountants may discover that the unexpectedly high bill is due to an error rather than the reason(s) above.

The Basics of Failure-to-File and Failure-to-Pay Penalties

Whether or not you can pay your tax bill, be sure to file your return by April 15th. Failure to file by this date results in a set of tax penalties separate from any interest, fees, and penalties that result from your inability to pay.

There are six critical points to be aware of when it comes to failure-to-file and failure-to-pay penalties:

1. One set of penalties is assessed for failure to file by April 15th. A separate set of penalties is assessed if you do not pay the full amount you owe by the deadline. The failure-to-file penalties are higher than the failure-to-pay penalties, so it is always in your best interests to file your return on time.

2. The penalty for late filing is typically 5 percent of the unpaid taxes for each month or portion of a month past the filing deadline. This penalty starts to accrue on the first day after the filing deadline, and it is capped at 25 percent of your unpaid taxes.

3. You can avoid a failure to file penalty by submitting an extension request and paying at least 90 percent of the amount you owe.

4. The failure-to-pay penalty is typically .5 percent—half of one percent—of your unpaid taxes. This penalty is assessed each month or portion of a month past the filing deadline, and it starts to accrue on the first day after the filing deadline. This is also capped at 25 percent.

5. If you do not file on time and you fail to pay the amount you owe, the maximum combined penalty for both is 5 percent/month.

6. If your return is more than 60 days late, the minimum penalty is $135 or 100 percent of the unpaid taxes, whichever is less.

Clearly, no matter how bad your tax situation looks, the most important first step is filing your return. This keeps your bill from increasing dramatically while you explore payment options.

What to Expect After You File

If you file your return with a balance due and you fail to make a payment, the IRS will begin its collections process. Within a few months of filing, you will receive a letter that lists the amount you owe, along with any penalties and interest that have been applied. Review this letter carefully with a professional to ensure that the amounts match your records. The IRS can make mistakes, and you must call right away to report any discrepancies.

If you have not paid the bill, you will periodically receive additional letters from the IRS. This list shows your updated amount due, including additional penalties and interest that have accrued. The letters will offer you payment options, and they typically include the forms necessary to request an installment agreement. You may receive up to five letters with this information before the IRS moves forward with additional action to collect the outstanding amount.

Often, the next letter you receive comes by certified mail, and it notifies you of the agency's intent to file a Notice of Federal Tax Lien. Such a Notice is filed with your local Secretary of State or County Recorder's office, and it is essentially makes your debt a matter of public record. When you have a Notice of Federal Tax Lien on file, you are unable to sell or borrow against your major assets, such as real estate. The Federal Tax Lien asserts the government's legal claim to your property if you don't make appropriate payment arrangements.

You may have no intention of selling or borrowing against your assets, in which case you may not be concerned with the filing of a Notice of Federal Tax Lien. However, these Notices can have a lasting impact on your financial health. All of the major credit bureaus consider IRS actions in calculating your credit score, making it nearly impossible to obtain credit for future purchases. Worse still, once you pay your outstanding balance and the Notice is removed, the negative information will remain on your credit reports for seven to ten years.

Unfortunately, a Notice of Federal Tax Lien isn't the final step in the collections process. If you still do not pay, the IRS may eventually seize your assets and sell them to pay your tax bill, or the agency might levy your wages and bank accounts. The bottom line is that you will eventually have to pay. Doing nothing is the worst possible option when it comes to managing your tax debt.

Options for Resolving Tax Payment Obstacles

Your financial situation plays a major role in determining the best way to sort out tax issues, and there are a variety of IRS programs in place to make the payment process simpler for you. The fastest way to end your dealings with the IRS is to pay the amount you owe in full. For some, this means borrowing from friends, family, or financial institutions. Others choose to pay with credit cards. In certain situations, selling assets to pay the IRS is a logical solution.

Of course, paying in full isn't an option for many people who find themselves in this situation. If your circumstances do not allow you to pay in full, begin by contacting the IRS directly. Explain your situation and inquire about your options. Often, the agency will conduct a formal evaluation of your ability to pay, then offer you possible solutions based on the results of this evaluation. There following are four common paths to resolving outstanding tax debts.

Installment Agreement

If you cannot pay the entire amount you owe right away, the most popular choice is to request an Installment Agreement. While you are making payments through your Installment Agreement, collection activity stops. Your debt is divided into equal monthly payments, and you have an opportunity to influence the terms of the agreement as far as the amount of each payment and which day of the month payments are due.

Before applying for an Installment Agreement, double-check to be sure that you have filed all of your required tax returns. Installment agreements will not be granted if there are any returns missing. You should also keep in mind that if you overpay taxes and are due a refund in future years, the refund amount will be applied to your agreement.

Installment Agreements can be initiated online for individuals who owe $50,000 or less in taxes, penalties, and interest. Businesses that owe $25,000 or less in payroll taxes may also qualify for an online agreement. If you owe more than this amount, you can still apply for an Installment Agreement, but you must complete a separate set of paper-based forms that are available through the IRS or your Certified Tax Coach.

If you owe less than $25,000, you are unlikely to have any trouble qualifying for an Installment Agreement. If your bill is higher than $25,000, you may need to explore other possibilities. Entering into an Installment Agreement may remove tax liens and levies, but be aware that a missed payment can result in the entire amount becoming payable on demand.

You should also consider that one of the terms of an IRS Installment Agreement is your commitment to pay future taxes on time. If you expect to have another high balance due the year after you establish an Installment Agreement, start thinking about how you will pay it as soon as possible, as your agreement may be voided if you don't pay future tax bills on time.

Finally, it is important to note that fees apply to Installment Agreements, which will increase the total amount you owe. Effective January 1, 2017, basic Installment Agreement fees increased to $225. Additional fees may be assessed for changing the terms of your agreement. There are discounts available for low-income individuals and those who agree to have payments debited directly.

Offer in Compromise

While the IRS has a bad reputation, the truth is that the agency's goal is to work with you to find a solution that satisfies your debt without dramatically impacting your financial health. Offers in Compromise are an option for finding middle ground, so you can put your tax bill behind you. Through this process, the IRS examines your ability to pay, and it assesses whether a settlement is more cost-effective than continued collection activity.

Qualifying for an Offer in Compromise can be tricky, as there are strict criteria you must meet in terms of why you cannot or will not pay the full amount due. If financial hardship is the primary reason for your request to participate in this program, you can expect the IRS to apply a specific formula to calculate the amount of your settlement based on your total financial picture. Examples of factors that will be considered include assets, liabilities, and disposable income.

There are three reasons the IRS may consider an Offer in Compromise:

1. **Questions on Liability** – If there is some doubt about whether you owe the amount stated, you have an opportunity to explain why you think the assessment is incorrect. You may be granted an Offer in Compromise if you make a compelling case.

2. **Financial Hardship** – The most common reason people apply for an Offer in Compromise is financial hardship. If there are serious doubts as to whether the total debt can ever be paid, and you can illustrate financial hardship through the application materials, you may qualify.

3. **Effective Tax Administration** – Some individuals in dire financial straits or business may have the ability to pay or an ability to pay more than what they offer. However, if they can show that, despite the fact that they owe taxes and the taxes were assessed appropriately, requiring payment would be unfair as it would create extreme financial hardship.

Note that you will not be considered for an Offer in Compromise unless you have filed all required tax returns, and that there is a fee for this service. When you complete your Offer in Compromise application, you will have an option of two payment methods. You can either pay in full upon acceptance of the offer, or you can set up monthly installment payments until the total agreed-upon amount is paid. If you select the option to pay in full, include 20 percent of the total offer you are making with your application. If you select the Installment Agreement, include your first payment with the application.

Currently Not Collectible

Those facing financial hardship may qualify for Currently Not Collectible status, which is another route to stopping IRS collection activity. In this situation, the government agrees that you simply do not have the ability to pay the taxes you owe. Individuals in Currently Not Collectible status typically do not own any assets that can be levied, and their income is just enough to cover basic necessities.

Note that Currently Not Collectible is a temporary status; it doesn't exempt you from paying your bill if your circumstances change. In fact, the IRS will continue to follow up on your financial situation to see if it has improved. Generally, these follow-ups are conducted annually, and you will be expected to pay as soon as you have the means to do so.

Bankruptcy

- If your circumstances are truly dire, you might be considering bankruptcy. In limited situations, outstanding tax debt can be discharged through bankruptcy proceedings. There are five criteria you must meet to qualify for elimination of tax debt through bankruptcy:
- The debt must consist of income taxes. Payroll tax liability, fraud penalties, and trust fund taxes are not eligible for discharge.
- You are not involved in tax evasion or fraud-related crimes.
- You cannot include taxes in bankruptcy proceedings if they were assessed less than 240 days before you filed for bankruptcy.
- Any taxes included in the bankruptcy resulted from tax returns that were filed at least two years before the bankruptcy filing.
- The taxes came due three years before you filed for bankruptcy. This timeframe includes all relevant extensions.

If you determine that bankruptcy is the most appropriate way to solve your tax problems, check and double-check these dates before filing for bankruptcy. Be sure that your legal counsel is aware of your tax situation, and consider discussing your plans with your Certified Tax Coach. Filing for bankruptcy just a little too soon can mean none of your tax debt is eligible for discharge.

Allowable Expenses

Most of these options rely on your ability to demonstrate financial hardship, so it is important to understand what the IRS considers in calculating your living expenses versus your disposable income. The agency relies on a policy titled Collection Financial Standards, which offers guidance in determining your ability to pay.

The standards define which expenses are considered critical to the health and welfare of you and your family, as well as which expenses are necessary for the production of household income. Some of these include food, clothing, housing, utilities, transportation, and medical expenses. For example, the monthly food allowance is calculated as follows:

- One person: $345 per month
- Two people: $612 per month
- Three people: $737 per month
- Four people: $845 per month

An additional $345 per month is added for each additional person in the household.

The standards are created from regional and national databases that track average costs of these goods and services, and the entire set of standards is available online through the IRS website. These amounts are adjusted annually so.

The benefit of standardizing these types of expenses is that you don't have to prove how much you actually spend on necessities. You automatically qualify for the entire allowance relevant to your family size without producing receipts and other documentation. In most cases, family size is based on the number of exemptions you claim on your tax returns. Of course, if your expenses are higher than the standard allowances, you will be required to document your actual expenses and explain why you should be credited at a higher-than-average rate.

Requesting a First Time Penalty Abatement

If this is the first time you have been unable to pay your taxes on time, the IRS may consider an administrative First Time Penalty Abatement of the penalties you were assessed. This relief can apply to penalties for failing to file, failing to pay on time, and/or failing to deposit taxes when due. The eligibility criteria include the following:

- You were not required to file a return or you were not assessed any penalties in the three years prior to the year for which you are requesting the Abatement.
- All of your returns have now been properly filed, or you have completed appropriate extension requests.
- You have paid or arranged to pay all taxes due.

Because the failure-to-pay penalties accrue until your taxes are paid in full, it is wise to request an Abatement once you have finished paying the entire principal balance. You can then make a request based on the full amount of the penalty assessed.

Final Thoughts on Overcoming Obstacles in the Tax Maze

Installment Agreements, Offers in Compromise, Currently Not Collectible, Bankruptcy and First Time Penalty Abatements are the most common ways to resolve tax bills when you cannot pay the full amount due. However, there is an additional caveat that you should keep in mind.

The IRS only has ten years to collect your overdue taxes, interest, and penalties. While there are exceptions to this rule, in most cases the statute of limitations applies based on the date the taxes were first assessed. While it is quite unlikely that the IRS will simply overlook your outstanding tax debt for ten years, it is an important point to bear in mind when collection activity drags on for many years.

Keep in mind that there are always con artists who want to take advantage of other people's desperate circumstances, and IRS-related scams are quite common. Don't rely on too-good-to-be-true promises from disreputable companies that offer guarantees that you will qualify for an IRS program. In fact, there are absolutely no companies that can make such a guarantee. Instead, trust your Certified Tax Coach to guide you through your options when you have an issue with paying your entire tax bill by the due date.

Sources

- https://www.irs.gov/newsroom/eight-facts-on-late-filing-and-late-payment-penalties
- https://www.irs.gov/payments/offer-in-compromise
- https://www.irs.gov/payments/payment-plans-installment-agreements
- https://www.irs.gov/businesses/small-businesses-self-employed/collection-financial-standards
- https://www.irs.gov/businesses/small-businesses-self-employed/national-standards-food-clothing-and-other-items
- https://www.irs.gov/businesses/small-businesses-self-employed/penalty-relief-due-to-first-time-penalty-abatement-or-other-administrative-waiver
- https://www.irs.gov/irm/part5/irm_05-016-001r.html

ABOUT THE AUTHOR

David Stone, EA

IRS Solutions™ was founded in 1998 by David Stone, Enrolled Agent. David worked for the Internal Revenue Service for 12 years. During this time, he grew tired of seeing uninformed taxpayers be taken advantage of and get the runaround. He found dishonest accountants giving false promises troublesome as well. As an Enrolled Agent, David can represent clients nationwide in front of the IRS and most state agencies. The Federal Government holds him to a strict standard.

IRS Solutions™ has grown into a trustworthy company—a company that truly "has your back." We are committed to both the individual and small businesses to reduce tax liability to the lowest possible amount. Although we are located in Valencia, California, our clients are nationwide. We work with top professionals to assist in all matters. Please call our office and we'll show you how you can lower your tax and increase your profits.

IRS Solutions is located in Valencia, California, and David can be contacted online at www.irssolutions.com or by phone at (661) 775-6200.

CHAPTER 15

Forging Your Own Path: Getting Creative with Expense Deductions

BY T. SCOTT TERRY, CPA, CTC

After all the tax returns are filed, accountants can have some fun sharing stories with each other over the strangest deductions they saw clients attempt. The lengths people will go to save on taxes never disappoints. Every year, the Minnesota Society of CPAs (MNCPA) compiles a list of the most creative. In this chapter, you will learn about some of the most bizarre—and completely illegal—deductions that real people actually tried to file in Minnesota and across the country. You will also learn about some unusual deductions that are actually legal. Your Certified Tax Coach knows the difference and will make sure you get all the deductions you are entitled to—maybe even some wacky ones—while you and your business remain protected and within the law.

Improper Personal Expenses

- One unfortunate casino enthusiast tried to write off gambling losses as a charitable donation to the Minnesota State Lottery, while another attempted to deduct them as a donation to the casino itself. Neither qualified as charitable contributions under IRS regulations.

- While the daycare deduction is a huge benefit for working parents, season passes to an amusement park are not allowed as a daycare expense, though this is a pretty creative solution to childcare needs.

- For most people, there is no need to specify that the child care credit is intended for human children, but one extra creative dog owner disagreed. He felt his pet suffered extreme anxiety as a result of being left home while he went to work, so he attempted to deduct dog-walker expenses under the child care category. As you can imagine, the IRS didn't see things the same way, and this taxpayer had to pay back taxes.

- There are plenty of generous education credits, but school lunches are not included, especially when your children are in grades K-12.

- Though they certainly take their places as members of the family, dogs and cats simply cannot be claimed as dependents. A shocking number of people list pets as dependents each year, which is an absolute violation of IRS regulations. Along those same lines, pet adoption fees cannot be counted under adoption credit programs.

- Expenses related to your family dog are not deductible, even if you count on your furry companion as your primary home security system.

- Lending money to friends and family is pretty risky, and the IRS is not willing to take on any of that risk. Sadly, no matter how much you handed over to your loved ones, you can't claim a loss if they don't pay you back.

- Claiming unqualified dependents is one of the most common tax errors, and the IRS is familiar with nearly every scheme. You can expect to hear from the tax courts if you try to fool the system. In one case, a woman decided that the young man who rented a room in her home was like family, and she claimed him as a dependent nephew on her tax return. It didn't take long for her story to come under scrutiny, and she ended up paying $5,000 in back taxes and a $2,000 fine.

Misplaced Medical Expenses

- No matter what you read in the news, the IRS does not agree that the fallout shelter you constructed can be itemized under preventative medicine. You also can't write off your new ATV as a medical expense because it provides stress relief.

- Though one might call a prostitute a consultant, the money spent is still not deductible. One New York lawyer found this out the hard way when he tried to claim $65,934 paid to prostitutes as medical expenses. He added on another $5,000 for pornography and sex therapy books, but he was unable to successfully prove any connection to treatment for a medical condition.

- Whether you try to deduct them as business or medical expenses, tattoos and piercings simply have no place on your tax return. Many have tried—and failed—to get these included, leaving them with hefty interest and penalty charges.

- One enterprising Massachusetts physician generously donated sperm for use in in-vitro fertilization. He tried to write off thousands of dollars in related expenses, but he was met with a resounding no from the IRS. Because he had no medical condition preventing him from procreating naturally, the donations were completely optional. The tax court determined that costs associated with donating sperm were a personal expense.

- In another sperm donation related case, a Manhattan man attempted to take a depletion allowance for his contributions. Again, the IRS did not recognize this as a legitimate tax deduction.

Unacceptable Business Expenses

- Unless you are working in very specific types of jobs, designer clothing is not a permitted business expense. Deductible work-related costs include ordinary and necessary business expenses only, even if looking nice gets you further with sales. The same goes for plastic surgery and personal grooming tools. You simply can't deduct your manicures and pedicures, unless you can prove that they are required to conduct business.

- Putting stickers or magnets on your car to advertise your business might be a great way to build your reputation, but it doesn't make all of your vehicle expenses deductible as marketing costs. The stickers and magnets might qualify, though.

- There are all kinds of reasons why hiring family members makes sense tax wise, but don't cross the line. If you are ever audited, you can be sure that this will be one of the first areas to undergo careful scrutiny. Far too many people have been caught trying to pass off infant family members as business employees, with dire consequences as far as interest and penalties.

- More than once, enterprising parents of newlyweds—or the newlyweds themselves—have tried to deduct all of the expenses related to their wedding. Considering the average cost of a wedding is $35,329, it's no wonder taxpayers are looking for a break. However, no matter how many of the guests are business related, this is not a business expense.

- A physician attending a medical seminar in Hawaii took his wife along for the trip, and then tried to deduct the expense of her snorkeling lessons. His logic was that he wouldn't have incurred the expense but for his attendance at the seminar, but the IRS didn't see things the same way.

- While dentures may qualify for deduction when itemized with your other medical expenses, they cannot be claimed as a business expense, even if, as one taxpayer claimed, they were necessary to improve his enunciation in his profession as an actor.

- Reasonable entertainment expenses qualify as business deductions, as long as business is conducted during the event. However, reasonable is defined fairly conservatively. In one case, a business owner hosted clients at the Super Bowl, then tried to deduct the expense. Because it was over-the-top entertainment, it didn't meet the standard for reasonable entertainment expense.

Illegal Expenses

- This final point should go without saying, but sadly, common sense doesn't always prevail: if an activity is illegal, it cannot be counted as a deductible expense on your taxes. One Pittsburgh business owner got himself into hot water with the IRS and law enforcement when he forgot this basic principle. His store was failing, so he decided to hire an arsonist to burn the facility down so he could collect the insurance. He might have gotten away with it if he hadn't tried to claim the fee he paid to the arsonist as a business expense.

- Along those lines, you can't deduct your speeding tickets or parking tickets, even if you get them while rushing to a business meeting.

All of these are good for a chuckle—and none are legitimate deductions—but they might be inspired by some of the unusual tax deductions that you actually can take.

The Medical Deductions You May Be Missing Out On

Generally, if you have a diagnosed medical condition that requires care, the related expenses qualify under medical deduction regulations. That means some cosmetic procedures can be included in your itemized medical expenses. Though the procedures might fall under the heading of cosmetic surgery, they are corrective in nature, not solely for the purpose of improving your appearance.

Corrective cosmetic surgery is defined as medically necessary to remedy disfigurements resulting from congenital abnormalities, personal injuries, or disfiguring diseases. This area of the tax code can get a bit murky. The following examples will help you navigate the cosmetic surgery area of the maze.

After losing significant amounts of weight, many individuals are left with excess skin. The cost of removing it is often classified as elective cosmetic surgery, because it is not a medical necessity. However, if the skin is causing health problems such as frequent infections, you are far more likely to have the option of deducting surgery expenses on your tax return.

Breast augmentation is a popular cosmetic procedure, but it is almost never medically necessary. However, there is an exception to this rule. Breast cancer survivors and individuals with other conditions that require reconstruction of the breasts can deduct expenses related to this procedure.

Surgery and medical care for gender reassignment could be deductible in whole or in part under specific circumstances. Typically, you can deduct procedures that are considered corrective for treatment of diagnosed gender identity conditions. However, you may discover that while the gender reassignment surgery itself is covered, breast augmentation is not.

Of course, cosmetic surgery isn't the only area of medicine in which allowable deductions get complicated. Taxpayers frequently attempt to deduct equipment and supplies related to their hobbies under the heading of stress relief. As aforementioned, the IRS has no intention of subsidizing ATVs, and many people have tried and failed to deduct dance lessons as treatment for everything from varicose veins and arthritis to nervous disorders.

That doesn't mean you should stop thinking creatively about your medical expenses, though. Some unusual deductions are absolutely legitimate. For example, one man was able to deduct the cost of his new swimming pool and the expenses related to its upkeep after being diagnosed with emphysema. His doctor told him that low-impact exercise was important for treating the disease, and the IRS agreed.

Business Travel Deductions

If you tend to be quite cautious with your business travel deductions, you might be missing out on certain allowable expenses. For example, when you travel to attend a seminar or educational opportunity related to your business, there are often excursions included in the itinerary. Even if the excursions appear to be for entertainment purposes rather than business-related, they may still be deductible. Check the seminar brochure to see how the event is listed. Outings listed as networking opportunities or meet-and-greets may qualify as legitimate deductions since they are sponsored by the seminar provider. Just be sure to keep the brochure and receipts in case questions come up.

Even the most unusual travel experiences may qualify for deduction if they are related to your business. For example, one couple who owned a dairy successfully deducted expenses for an African Safari. They had enough documentation to demonstrate that the safari was an important research opportunity for operation of the business.

Essentially, any unreimbursed business travel expenses that fall under the heading of ordinary and required—airfare, fuel charges, and parking fees, for example—can qualify as business expenses if the amount exceeds a certain percentage of your income. Consult your Certified Tax Coach to learn more about which business travel deductions apply to you.

The Intersection of Medical Expenses and Business Expenses

Every year, there are new stories of odd medical expenses that taxpayers have tried to pass off as business-related. As previously mentioned, elective cosmetic surgery is typically on the Not Eligible list, despite the argument that looking better improves the odds of getting a job, making sales, and generally increasing income. However, there are exceptions to this rule.

In one case, a stripper's breast augmentation surgery was approved as a legitimate business expense, as they were proven to be "stage props." This was a rare situation in which the enhanced size vastly exceeded any ordinary breast augmentation, and the implants were so disruptive to the individual's personal life and comfort that she planned to have them removed once she left the adult entertainment business.

In another case, the owner of a wine shop deducted expenses related to surgery that would correct his sense of smell as a business expenses. He was able to successfully argue that the surgery was critical to his business, as his sense of smell was important for properly examining the wines he sold to his clients.

The key here is to ensure you have the documentation to support the relationship between your work and your medical need. You have to establish that the treatment is linked to your ability to generate income and, if you are claiming a business expense, you must establish that you wouldn't incur the cost of the treatment but for your work.

Unexpected Allowable Business Expenses

Although you are expected to arrive at work fully clothed, the IRS is not generally willing to subsidize your wardrobe. Your clothes are considered a personal expense, and if you choose to spend your money on designer brands, you have to absorb the entire cost, even if looking nice is better for your career. However, there are exceptions to every rule.

One member of Rod Stewart's band successfully argued that his leather pants, hat, and vest were part of his on-stage persona. Under the same logic that makes required costumes business-related, he was able to deduct them. Unfortunately, his attempt at using the same argument for deducting the cost of his silk underwear was met with skepticism and ultimately denied.

As discussed, expenses related to pets are not permitted, but there are exceptions for some working dogs and cats. Businesses that use certain breeds of dogs as part of their security plan, for example junkyards, impound lots, and similar, might have an argument for claiming some of their dog-related costs as a business expense. Dog breeders who claim the income they receive from puppy sales may also be able to deduct certain dog-related expenses.

In one memorable case, a shop with significant rodent issues successfully deducted some of the expenses related to their cat, after every other mouse control solutions failed and the cat's hunting prowess reduced the amount of stock lost to mice. In a similar scenario, junkyard owners put out food for feral cats in an attempt to draw them onto the property at night. The cats were instrumental in reducing the snake and rat population on the property, making it safer for staff and customers. The IRS conceded that the cost of the cat food was a deductible business expense.

Be cautious when claiming credits for pet-related expenses. One enterprising landscaper used his dog to pull heavy lawn tools around. He thought this qualified the care of his dog as a deductible business expense. The tax courts disagreed, and he had to pay the taxes owed for the improper business expense.

While meals and personal care items don't typically qualify as business expenses, there are occasions in which these items can be directly connected with your income. One body builder claimed a variety of costs associated with his profession, including $4,000 in buffalo meat, tanning products, and posing oil. His argument was that his profession required him to consume significant amounts of protein, which caused him to eat at least three pounds of buffalo meat a day. The IRS wasn't willing to approve the buffalo meat deduction, but the tanning products and posing oil were considered legitimate business expenses.

When taking any business expense, you should carefully document the link between the costs you incur and income you generate. This is especially important when you are claiming unusual deductions. One couple found this out the hard way. Both worked for an airline, but said they made a little extra money on the side through the sale of eggs from their 20 chickens and feathers from their two emus. They tried to deduct the costs of owning chickens and emus as business expenses. Unfortunately, they never listed the egg and feather revenues on their income tax returns, so they were unable to convince the IRS that their business expenses were allowed under tax law.

Be sure to get professional guidance when it comes to unusual business expenses, as there is a fine line between what is allowed and what will get you into hot water. In some cases, the line is so faint, it is ridiculously easy to miss. Consider this apparently conflicting interpretation of tax regulations: in one case, a gas station owner was able to deduct the expense of beer that he gave away to his customers for free. However, when another business owner gave clients whiskey as a gift, the IRS said the cost of the liquor was absolutely not deductible.

Balancing Tax Savings Strategies with Audit Risk

When it comes to taking tax deductions, the bottom line is this: you are entitled to deduct expenses incurred in the operation of your business. Your Certified Tax Coach will work with you to determine whether specific expenses meet IRS requirements, and what documentation is required to protect you in case of an audit. Keep in mind that it is unwise to get too creative, as one inappropriate deduction can inspire the IRS to start digging through your entire return, and often they don't stop with the current year.

Penalties for filing returns with illegitimate deductions listed can be substantial. In addition to losing the deduction you tried to claim—and therefore becoming responsible for the related taxes, penalties, and interest—you may find yourself responsible for a 20 percent understatement penalty. In extreme cases, penalties for understatement of tax liability can be as high as 40 percent, and it is impossible to calculate the expenses related to the time and energy you will spend dealing with the IRS.

Too many odd deductions on your tax return can draw unwanted attention from the IRS. However, that doesn't mean you should pass on legitimate deductions that you are entitled to. Taking advantage of all available opportunities to lower your tax bill means more money in your pocket. Certified Tax Coaches can help you identify all of the deductions available to you, and they have the experience and expertise to keep you from running afoul of tax regulations.

Sources

- https://www.accountingweb.com/tax/individuals/10-strange-tax-deductions-the-irs-will-frown-upon
- https://www.mncpa.org/publications/footnote/2016-02/MNC-PA-outrageous-tax-deductions.aspx
- https://www.prnewswire.com/news-releases/mncpa-issues-list-of-strange-and-unusual-tax-deductions-244854181.html
- https://www.usatoday.com/story/travel/2013/04/08/whats-a-legitimate-business-travel-deduction/2064657/
- https://www.irs.gov/irm/part20/irm_20-001-005#idm140180800831616
- https://turbotax.intuit.com/tax-tips/fun-facts/7-of-the-craziest-illegal-tax-deductions-ever-claimed/L3ZElWEFZ
- http://www.smbiz.com/sbfaq022.html
- http://fortune.com/2017/02/03/wedding-cost-spending-usa-average/
- https://www.forbes.com/sites/peterjreilly/2012/07/20/julian-block-on-cosmetic-surgery-as-a-business-expense/#18020a31736f

ABOUT THE AUTHOR

T. Scott Terry, CPA, CTC

Scott is the founder and managing member of TST Accounting, LLC in Tomball, Texas. As a Certified Tax Coach, Scott works with business owners and investors to carefully structure their business activities to legally minimize their tax burdens while maximizing their liability protections. This is accomplished through proactive tax planning—using court tested strategies to arrange activities in the most tax efficient manner.

Scott is also the founder and CEO of New Day Tax Resolution, LLC. At New Day, he helps troubled taxpayers settle significant IRS problems and get back into the tax "system." We find that troubled taxpayers can sometimes benefit significantly from incorporating some tax planning strategies into their lives going forward. This reduces their future tax obligations and helps them stay in compliance with the IRS.

Prior to founding TST and New Day, Scott spent many years in financial leadership roles in several fast growing, small to medium sized businesses. He has extensive experience in raising capital, setting up financial systems, policies, and procedures, and running businesses. While varied, Scott's experience has primarily been in the areas of construction and manufacturing with a specialty in long term construction contracts with percentage of completion revenue recognition. Scott loves to use his "real world" business experience to help his clients, even outside of the areas of accounting or tax compliance.

Scott's first college degree was in Electrical Engineering and he spent the first ten years of his career in Engineering roles, primarily with Compaq Computer and then Hewlett Packard. He began to get more interested in the business aspects of those companies, so night classes at the

University of Houston became part of his weekly routine. Scott earned his MBA and then a Master's Degree in Accountancy at U of H. Scott moved into the finance organization at Hewlett Packard before moving on to financial leadership roles in smaller businesses.

You can reach Scott by phone at (281) 246-4421 or by e-mail at sterry@tstcpa.com.

CHAPTER 16

Finding the Right Accountant to Successfully Guide You Through the Tax Maze

BY JOSEPH D. ROSE, CPA, CTC

C hoosing an accountant takes time, and you might consider for-going this process in favor of a do-it-yourself approach. It can be tempting to file your own taxes. After all, there are ample websites, manuals, and books devoted to DIY tax returns. However, most people who go this route end up regretting it for good reason: the tax savings they miss out on costs them much more money than a good accountant would have. Even if you are a licensed accountant yourself, hiring a professional guide to take you through the tax maze can prevent you from falling into common DIY traps.

Focus on Your Core Mission

Businesses that take on too many extraneous activities often find their resources stretched thin. It is common for these companies to re-organize by outsourcing any functions that detract from their core mis-sion. Securing third-party vendors to manage human resources issues, IT support, and security responsibilities are just a few examples.

Individuals can easily find themselves in a similar situation when they take time and energy from pursuing their primary goals to work on unrelated projects. You may well be capable of handling your own tax returns, but the time you invest could be better spent on other things. Consider how much each hour of your time is worth—and how many hours you will devote to learning new accounting skills and trying to apply them successfully. Then double that figure, because your estimate is almost always too low. The cost of managing your own taxes is typically much higher than the expense of hiring a professional.

Avoid Missed Opportunities for Tax Savings

The tax code is a massive and constantly changing body of knowledge. It seems like there are new deductions available every year. At the same time, strategies that have been available to you for decades can suddenly end without warning. Licensed accountants and Certified Tax Coaches stay on top of the changes, and they know how current tax laws apply to your unique situation. Without their guidance, you are likely to miss out on some of the most lucrative opportunities for tax savings.

Accountants and Certified Tax Coaches can enhance your tax strategy in other ways as well. As a result of their extensive experience in the field, they have a solid understanding of what works, and just as important, what doesn't. You can count on these qualified professionals to steer you in the right direction when it comes to long-term strategies. For instance, they can offer advice on how to structure your business, whether you should consider cost segregation, and how to best expand your company without incurring significant tax liability.

A Second Opinion for Creative Tax Savings

While accountants and Certified Tax Coaches are helping you choose the best strategies for your business, they are also performing another vital function: keeping you out of trouble with the IRS. There are a variety of ways you can legally push the limits in terms of what you deduct, but far too many people cross the line. Unfortunately, if you get too creative with your tax savings attempts, you can find yourself liable for additional taxes, interest, and penalties.

Tax professionals have experience in dealing with the IRS, and they know what has worked and what has failed for other clients. They keep up with case law to better understand how tax courts view certain types of deductions, and if they don't know an answer, they know where to find it. They have networks of tax experts that they can rely on for advice, and they often have connections with accounting related professional organizations. All of this comes with years of experience in the field, which you cannot duplicate in a do-it-yourself situation.

Tax law is one of the most complex sets of regulations nationwide, so don't try to find your way through the maze alone. Hiring tax experts is worth every penny, and it is far more likely that you will realize generous tax savings with their assistance than if you choose to go it alone.

Making the Right Match

It doesn't matter how much or how little you make. You deserve an accountant that has the experience and expertise to keep your tax bills as low as possible. Finding the right match can be a challenge, but the effort is well worth your while. These tips will ensure that you get through the tax maze with your wealth intact.

Tax Savings Techniques

Exploring every possible twist and turn in the tax maze isn't for everyone. There are plenty of accountants who prefer a straightforward path to completing returns. The first question to ask when reviewing your options is whether the potential accountant's philosophies match your own. At the most fundamental level, the following three techniques are go-to strategies for saving money on taxes.

Shifting Money from High Tax Categories to Low Tax Categories

How you come into money is just as important as how much you have, and different categories of income and wealth are taxed in very different ways. Accountants and Certified Tax Coaches are experienced in choosing the right strategy to minimize your tax liability. For example, it may be wise to shift funds from high tax areas like income to lower tax areas like investing. With investments, moving money around can make a significant difference. You may even be able to realize savings by building an entirely new business.

As you get to know the accountants you are considering to manage your finances, try to learn more about how comfortable they are with giving advice on shifting funds from high tax categories to low tax categories. Do they offer suggestions, or do they simply work with the information you provide? Your ideal guide will offer experience-based assistance to maximize your tax savings.

Timing Strategies for Best Possible Impact

If you spend any time with investors, you know that timing the market is critical to bringing in profit. The same goes for minimizing tax liability. The best accountants can not only give you advice on your portfolio, but they can also make recommendations on when and how to take deductions for optimal tax reduction. When speaking with potential accountants, ask about their experience and level of comfort with giving timing advice. Do they have a history of working with clients in this area? Knowing when and how to use the tax regulations to your advantage can dramatically change your total tax bill.

Deep Understanding of Tax Law

Endless changes in tax regulations create and close loopholes at a dizzying rate. Keeping up with case law and legislation activities is a full-time job. Fortunately, for the best accountants, staying current with tax law is a high priority, so you don't have to worry about all of the changes if you have the right advisor. Choose an accountant that is current on new legislation and how laws are applied in real-world scenarios. Their intimate knowledge of when and how certain methods can be legally used should surpass your own, saving you a bundle on your tax bill.

As with investors and business owners, accountants have varying levels of tolerance for risk. Some are more creative than others. The secret for getting great tax advice is to choose an accountant whose philosophies match your own. Your accountant's expertise in shifting money, timing the use of tax strategies, and applying tax law should be deep and thorough, and willingness to think outside the box and employ creative tax savings strategies should mirror your personal views.

The Nuts and Bolts of Accounting Skills

Accountants must pass a grueling four part exam before they qualify for licensing in the state where they practice. After that, state Boards of Accountancy and national professional organizations require continuing professional education to maintain their license. That means that no matter who you hire, you can count on a certain basic level of knowledge and skill. However, basic knowledge is rarely enough if you want to pay the smallest possible amount on your tax bill. There are certain nuts and bolts questions to ask about a specific accountant's experience and expertise before handing over your financial information.

First, does the candidate have experience in your industry? This can change whether and how laws are applied to your personal situation, particularly if you own and operate a business. Accountants who primarily deal with personal returns may not know enough about business exemptions to maximize your tax savings, and those who usually work with sole proprietorships are unlikely to have the experience you need to manage taxes for a corporation. You can be sure that real estate businesses face very different tax issues from manufacturing businesses. Exemptions for a home day care are completely different from those claimed by restaurant owners. Whatever your profession, make sure that the accountant you hire is familiar with the industry and special circumstances that may apply to you.

Next, consider the sort of guidance you expect from your accountant. Some are skilled at completing and filing returns, but they prefer to stay away from advising on long-term strategies. If you have other professionals dedicated to your long-term goal achievement, you may want an accountant who stays focused on getting your return filed. However, if alternative resources are limited, it is important to hire an accountant who understands your goals and can confidently advise you on how best to achieve them.

The difference between tax preparation and tax planning is outlined below.

Tax Preparation Responsibilities

- Manages the process of filing returns at the end of the year.
- Handles your taxes reactively, working with figures that represent income you have already earned, investments you have already made, and money you have already spent.
- Reduces tax liability primarily through shifting expenses between categories.

Tax preparers do not often suggest ways to save on future taxes, as they deal with the money you have already spent. They take a historical perspective when it comes to your taxes, and their expertise lays in combining where you have been with where you are right now.

Any licensed CPA or accountant should be able to handle this task, and hiring a tax preparer is appropriate for individuals with simple tax situations. For example, if all of your income is earned through salary or wages at a regular job, a tax preparer can probably meet your needs. However, if you are self-employed or own a business, or if you do any sort of investing, proactive tax planning should be an important part of the services provided by your accountant.

Owning real estate also changes the type of service you need. Buying, maintaining, and selling property can result in significant tax liability, but with proper planning, it may be a technique for minimizing taxes instead. Experienced tax planning professionals—like Certified Tax Coaches—understand how to use tax regulations to your advantage.

Tax Planning Responsibilities

- Looks forward to proactively plan for minimizing taxes in the future.

- Offers advice on which purchases and investments you should make to reduce tax liability in the long term.

- Frequently reviews changes in tax law and applies new regulations as needed for an up-to-date tax strategy.

Accounting professionals typically require additional education and licensing to provide effective tax planning advice, since taking a proactive approach requires a unique skill set. While managing the past and present, they are also looking ahead to your financial future, so they can help you take action now to lower your tax liability later.

If you want a tax planner, look for an accountant who is proactive rather than reactive, one who focuses on tax planning as much as tax preparation. In addition to offering services once a year when it is time to file your taxes, this individual should stay updated on changes in the law and changes in your life. This ensures that you have the skilled professional you need to guide you through the tax maze. New regulations can make a method obsolete, requiring an adjustment to your tax strategy. Life changes may also mean an adjustment is in order. For example, getting married or having a child means you must regard your financial situation in an entirely different way.

Many taxpayers look at the difference in fees between a tax preparer and a tax planner and try to save money by paying only the lower rates charged by tax preparers. Unfortunately, this expense minimization plan rarely works. A proactive approach to tax strategy saves a significant amount in taxes you pay to the government, often far more than the difference in fees between tax preparers and tax planners.

Great Minds Think Alike

Simply looking at experience and knowledge isn't enough if you want to find the right match. How accountants apply regulations and their approach to minimizing tax liability can vary widely. If your personal philosophy doesn't match the philosophy of the accountant you choose, you can expect to find yourself at constant odds, and you certainly won't reach your financial goals.

Talk with potential accountants about their views on tax liability. If your expectation is that they apply every available tax minimization strategy to keep your bill as low as possible, you don't want to hire an accountant that operates under the philosophy that using tax loopholes is somehow unethical. Many people—including some accountants—believe that each taxpayer should pay his or her fair share without possibly going overboard to avoid tax expense. If you aren't aligned with this approach, you should keep looking to find a better match.

Explore how comfortable your potential accountant is with outside-the-box thinking. Remember, inappropriate conduct brings consequences for tax professionals as well as for you. Some accountants are unwilling to risk drawing criticism from the IRS with anything that is even slightly unorthodox, and they are not prepared to defend strategies that apply the law creatively. If you want an accountant who is open to hearing your ideas and is comfortable offering some unusual suggestions, be sure you don't hire a stickler for the straight and narrow path.

Determine whether the individual you are considering has as much respect for your expertise as you have for theirs. You are hiring your accountant to provide guidance in tax-related matters, and it goes without saying that you should choose someone you can rely on to know more about tax-related topics than you do. However, that doesn't take away from your knowledge and experience when it comes to your business. No long term relationship with an accountant will work if he or she fails to respect your knowledge in your own areas of expertise. Your relationship is a partnership, with each of you providing input, and your accountant should be on board with this perspective for long-term success.

Pay attention to how much time the prospective accountant spends with you. Does the appointment feel rushed, or is the accountant willing to spend time answering your questions? More important, are you being asked questions, too? Since you aren't an expert in all of the nuances of tax law, you are relying on your accountant to guide you. That means they have to ask questions to understand your situation and to identify potential deductions you haven't thought to mention. For example, certain athletic facilities qualify as business deductions when your employees are the primary users. However, if you don't know to mention that you installed a pool or gym for your staff—and your accountant doesn't ask—you are going to miss out on significant tax savings. Choose an accountant who gives you undivided attention and takes the time to explore all opportunities to save you money.

Finally, your personal comfort level with your accountant is as important as any of the other criteria listed. You are sharing intimate details of your financial situation, and you will be spending time together bouncing tax strategies off of one another. If you simply don't get along, whether because your personalities aren't matched or because you have underlying philosophical differences, move on. You cannot reach your financial goals if you don't trust your guide.

Certified Tax Coaches: Planning for Success

Creating a team of financial specialists can maximize your tax savings, as these individuals bring a variety of skills to address all aspects of your unique situation. Certified Tax Coaches make essential contributions to your long-term financial success by offering knowledge and support you simply can't get from other types of tax professionals. These are some of the traits and skills that Certified Tax Coaches provide:

- When candidates for the Certified Tax Coach program join, they commit to the principles of a specific school of thought as far as tax planning. They focus on being proactive rather than reactive, and they are philosophically aligned with the creative thinking discussed in this book.

- Certified Tax Coaches are specially trained in taking a proactive approach to tax savings, so they do much more than simply manage this year's returns. They look at your situation holistically, closely examining your long-term goals to create a plan that helps you get there.

- Unlike typical CPAs and accountants, Certified Tax Coaches tend to be entrepreneurial in spirit. They pursue the designation because they enjoy getting creative when it comes to designing and implementing tax planning strategies, and they make the extra effort to research and apply lesser known and more complex tax saving solutions.

- Because Certified Tax Coaches are available nationwide, you have greater flexibility in securing the support you need for tax planning. You aren't tied to a single firm with a specific accountant. You can be confident that any Certified Tax Coach you hire is well-versed in taking a proactive approach to your tax strategy and continuing to do so year-round.

Choosing who to trust with your finances, including your tax filing and tax minimization strategy, is one of the most important decisions you can make. How your accountant or Certified Tax Coach handles your individual income, investments, and expenses can make a dramatic difference in the amount of money you pay in taxes every year. Make sure more of your funds stay in your pocket by selecting the most qualified person for the job—one whose methods and philosophies will help you achieve your goals.

ABOUT THE AUTHOR

Joseph D. Rose, CPA, CTC

Joseph is the president and founder of Rose Tax Consulting. He is a Certified Tax Coach helping individuals and businesses in the Tucson and surrounding area reduce their tax burden with proactive strategies for over twenty years.

Joseph is a graduate of the University of Arizona with a Bachelor of Science in Business Administration majoring in Accounting. He is licensed in Arizona as a Certified Public Accountant and is a member in good standing with both the American Institute of Certified Public Accountants and the Arizona Society of Certified Public Accountants.

Joseph began his professional career as a controller of Envirocycle Management Service Technologies, a Tucson Arizona based engineering firm. He simultaneously implemented a strategic plan and began developing a tax business focused on helping small businesses navigate the complex world of income tax and reducing their tax burden.

Using his business experience and education, Joseph is in a perfect position to help small businesses improve operations by making the most of their resources. He also helps analyze strategies and opportunities which exist to help business owners maximize their tax savings.

Joseph is passionate about proactive tax planning being the key to reducing taxes. He has spent hundreds of hours of continuing education to ensure he provides the best solutions for his clients. Over the years Joseph has helped hundreds of business owners save hundreds of thousands in tax savings. He has given seminars on proactive tax planning as well as written a number of articles on the topic.

In addition to educating clients, Joseph generously supports several local charities with his time, knowledge and resources. He is very involved in his church having served on several committees and task forces. Joseph is married with four children and three grandchildren.

He can be reached at (855)836-4968 or by email at RoseTaxConsulting@gmail.com. You may also visit his website at www.desertrosetax.com.

Rose Tax Consulting
5702 East 22nd Street
Tucson, AZ 85711